THE
ACE OF CLUBS
A History of the Garrick

THE
ACE OF CLUBS

A History of the Garrick

RICHARD HOUGH

ANDRE DEUTSCH

First published 1986 by
André Deutsch Limited
105 Great Russell Street London WC1B 3LJ

Copyright © 1986 Richard Hough

All rights reserved

Typeset by Gloucester Typesetting Services
Printed in Great Britain by
St Edmundsbury Press, Bury St Edmunds, Suffolk

ISBN 0 233 97975 1

Contents

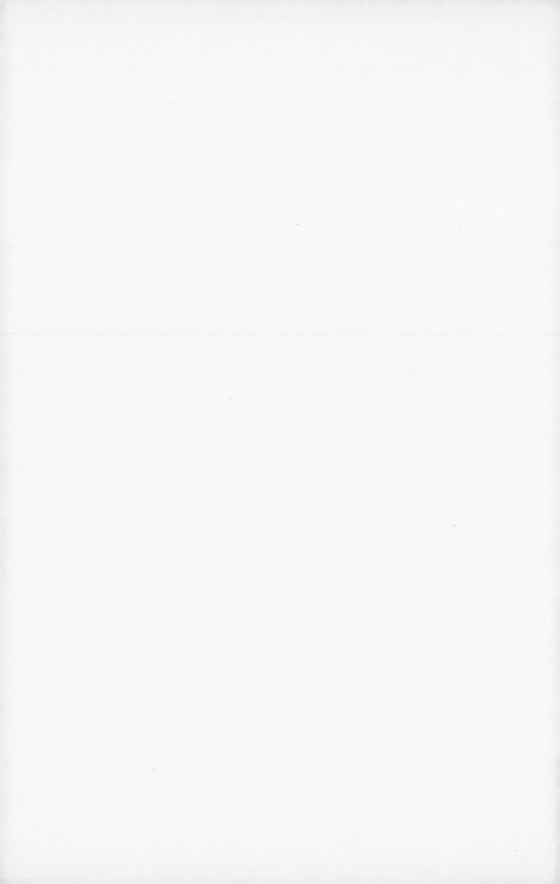

Illustrations

For the Staff

Acknowledgements

The author and publishers would like to thank the following for their kind permission to reproduce published copyright work: Sir Rupert Hart-Davis (*The Lyttleton-Hart-Davis Letters* vol vi); Malcolm Muggeridge (*The Infernal Grove*); Sir Robert Lusty (*Bound to be Read*); Sir John Gielgud (*An Actor in his Time*); William Collins, the publishers of *A Durable Fire: the letters of Duff and Diana Cooper 1913–1950*; The Bodley Head, publishers of *My Autobiography* by Charles Chaplin; and Faber and Faber, publishers of *Rose and Crown* by Sean O'Casey.

Author's Note

I wish to thank the Trustees for offering me this enjoyable task and the numerous Club members and members of the staff, and the Secretary, Martin Harvey, who have made it possible for me to carry it out by recounting tales and supplying memories of past members. I wish to single out the Right Honorable Sir Melford Stevenson (1931) who told me about the pre-Second World War Garrick; George Malcolm Thomson (1947) who knows the Baddeley period before Commander Satterthwaite RN (retd) took over as Secretary; Satters himself, who knows more about what went on in the '50s and '60s than anyone alive; and Tom Pocock (1959) who pre-dates me by a few years and as a writer himself was very helpful in an editorial capacity. Finally, Captain Jephthah West RN (retd) (1952) has done much beavering for me in the Garrick Library, and Marina Majdalany in the London Library; and Jackie Gumpert, my typist, who has once again rendered order out of chaos.

RICHARD HOUGH
August 1985

I

Bricks and Mortar

'There is a blessed home
Beyond this land of woe . . .'
HENRY WILLIAMS BAKER★

THE GARRICK CLUB has its roots deep in the need of actors, artists and writers for a venue, a private meeting place, for informal exchanges of view. They wanted good, preferably non-stop conversation in an atmosphere of cigar smoke (*never* pipes in clubs) and informed gossip in reasonable comfort and with a steady flow of drink.

At Brooks's when they were not bankrupting themselves at the gaming tables you could not, it was said, tell the living from the dead. The atmosphere at the Carlton (actually established a year after the Garrick) was 'like that of a Duke's house – with the Duke dead upstairs'. What conversation there was at White's was of such a low intellectual nature that grown men fell asleep both listening *and* talking. Worse still, the barriers were so rigid at White's that it was described as '*the* club from which people have died from exclusion . . . killed on the spot by a black ball; *the* club where, in dandy existence, either you must live or have no life'.[1]

Disraeli could not get elected to White's, and as for actors – at the Beefsteak it was accepted that they were disbarred simply by their profession and their low breeding. No other club was quite so openly prejudiced but none of the St James's clubs would contemplate accepting anyone connected with the stage, even if some (certainly mad or drunk) members were to propose him.

Literary men were also pariahs. 'They are considered as vermin in the fashionable clubs,' wrote one member of White's.

★ Not a member but written in the year when work started on the present club house.

All this led to the 'unwashed and filthy-fingered literati' setting up shop at the Athenaeum in 1823, and its members becoming referred to as 'of that philosophic dirty-shirt concern'.[2] But, now that this first step had been taken in this increasingly enlightened and prosperous age, what about Drama? What about that even more despised breed, the actors? They had nowhere to meet, no common ground where they could talk, professionally and generally, for the exchange of ideas and drinks, except the now somewhat debased coffee shops and noisy taverns.

This need was recognised in the late 1820s by a number of noble patrons of the theatre as well as the actors and managers themselves, and led to informal meetings to consider setting up a 'subscription house' for the dramatic arts. Clearly, the wealth and influence of the nobility would subsidise those who worked directly in the theatre.

'The time had come,' according to the Club's first Patron, 'when it would be an advantage to all concerned in literary industry, as well as society at large, if the Athenaeum were supplemented with a Club recruited from the most active caterers for the public taste with pen and pencil in the studio and on the stage'.[3]

As one newspaper correspondent put it (very ponderously) when the Club was in process of being formed, 'If . . . such men as the Duke of Sussex, the Duke of Devonshire, Lord Mulgrave, Lord Wharncliffe, and other persons of noble rank . . . really and efficiently join it [they did], so as to become the acquaintances, and possibly the friends and patrons, of meritorious dramatic writers and other men of genius, this might be a great encouragement and advantage to the latter, as well as a source of gratification, worthy of nobility and wealth, to the former.'[4] Indeed!

The Royal Family has not in recent years been widely regarded as energetic patrons of the theatre, so it is only fair to note that the foremost champion and inspirer of the Garrick Club, and its first Patron, was a member of the Royal Family – the Duke of Sussex. The Duke was the sixth son of George III, a mesmerist and the Grand Master of the United Grand Lodge of Freemasons as well, and it can be said that the Garrick has oblique Masonic as well as royal origins. That was in 1831; and the Club has enjoyed royal patronage ever since.

First public mention of the Garrick appears in October 1831, although the original decision to create the Club was earlier.

DRAMA
THE GARRICK CLUB

Under this name and under the auspices of many distinguished individuals, a new club is in progress of formation, the avowed purpose of which is the promotion of all the interests of the Drama. The subscribers, of whom 200 are to constitute the original nucleus, already amount to above 150; and a meeting is to take place this day to decide upon the further regulation, &c of the establishment. The only broad principles yet put forth are, that it is to combine all the purposes of a club with the advantages of a literary society, by bringing together the patrons of the Drama, and gentlemen who are most eminent in their respective circles.[5]

And now for the official definition and reason for founding the Club: '. . . in which actors and men of education and refinement might meet on equal terms', the distinction being clearly accepted. And the objects, as defined at the opening to the 'Rules of the Garrick Club', apply to this day:

THE GARRICK CLUB is instituted for the general patronage of the Drama; for the purpose of combining the use of a Club, on economical principles, with the advantages of a Literary Society; for bringing together the supporters of the Drama; and for the formation of a Theatrical Library, with works on Costume.

The members of the nobility made up about a third of the founder members, led by those mentioned above, Lord Kinnaird and Colonel Sir Andrew F. Barnard, equerry to George IV, both of them original Committee members, along with Samuel James Arnold, the manager of the Drury Lane theatre, Francis Mills, Henry Broadwood and Samuel Beazley, architect and dramatist. Then there was the Rev. Richard Harris Barham, author of *The*

Ingoldsby Legends, a spritely and outspoken fellow, who seems to have done most of the preliminary admin with his friend Mills – 'a very good-tempered *but* flighty man', as Barham described him.

The first informal meeting of the future Garrick took place at the Drury Lane Theatre, an appropriate womb for the Club if ever there was one, for David Garrick had directed its fortunes for twenty-nine years. The minutes are succinct: 'Present: Sir Andrew Barnard, Mr Mills, Mr Arnold and Mr Beazley, when a number of names were written down to be applied to, to join the Garrick Club as original members – Wednesday 17 August 1831.' There was another brief meeting – venue unstated – at 3 o'clock Saturday 27 August. A week later – and Saturday in that non-week-ending time became established for many decades as Garrick committee day – it was resolved that there should be two open committee meetings a week at number 3, Charles Street, Covent Garden.

By 7 September 1831 one hundred members had enrolled and it was decided that '. . . in future no name shall be inserted on the books without the sanction of three members present.' So there had been three free-for-all weeks when membership was offered more or less on the open market. From that time, like most clubs, you had to be invited and to be well supported to get in, a process which takes around six years today.

But at first it was all very happily casual. 'The Secretary reported that Mr Bartley met Mr Mills yesterday in James Street, Covent Garden, and said he had heard from Mr Pocock and that he desired his name to be put down as a member, and likewise Sir George Smart. Mr Cooke agreed to become a member, and proposed Mr Sidney Toore of Camden Town, known to Mr Wallack and Mr Harley, to be a member . . . Mr Greville proposed that the regulation of not making any further applications, be waived in the case of the Duke of Wellington . . .' – and so you would hope, a mere sixteen years after Waterloo.

The Garrick's eventual home was a constant preoccupation during these early and frequent meetings. Everyone agreed that the club should be established in the heart of theatreland, far removed from the swells and their snobbery in St James's, and one of Covent

[16]

Garden's numerous small hotels offered the most promising opportunity. On 10 September Mr Mills and the Secretary, Mr Winston, inspected Probatt's Hotel, 35 King Street, after learning 'that Mr Joy would let six rooms on the ground floor of the Grand Hotel, Covent Garden, Unfurnished, for one year, for Five Hundred Pounds'. A Mr Richardson offered 'the upper part of Drury House adjoining Richardson's Hotel, under the piazza, and by folding doors on the first floor, connect it to his hotel'.

There was a flurry of competition. On 20 October there was a brief inspection of Jeremy's House, Southampton Street, but 'all the rooms were small and inconvenient, the only large room was the shop which was below the staircase – very bad and the whole very much out of repair, the kitchen very dark and bad'.

Probatt had been asking £2,400; on 21 October he dropped the figure for the leasehold to £2,000. Richardson came back, too, offering a private door, three floors each containing four or five rooms, but no cellars, for £150 per annum. Mr Probatt won the day. '29 October 1831: Resolved that the Lease, furniture, Fixtures be (according to an inventory taken by Mr Machin) except the plate and linnen of Probatt's Hotel, No 35 King Street, Covent Garden be purchased for the sum of £1,500, the rent and taxes to be cleared to Michaelmas . . . In case the Bankers should refuse to advance the sum required, Mr Durrant offered to lend the money to be repaid as the subscriptions come in . . .'

Appropriate to its future rôle, number 35 had once been the home of the comedian William Lewis, 'whose elegance and affability earned him the sobriquet "Gentleman Lewis" '.[6] Lewis had made his debut in Dublin but from 1773 remained loyal to Covent Garden where he lived and worked until his death just thirty years before the Garrick moved into his old quarters.

While the formalities of purchase were being settled, there was the first proper meeting of the Club, the date being 15 October, 1831, at 3 o'clock. Lord Mulgrave was in the chair, and said this: 'The purpose of the Club being the general patronage of the Drama, By-Laws will be framed after the formation of the Club that will have for their end the promotion of all the objects contained in the original prospectus . . .' He certainly said much else, too; or at least one hopes so, and that it was of a lighter nature.

These rules were agreed: 'That the Club shall not exceed 300 members. That a Committee shall be nominated at the first General Meeting of 24 members in whom shall be invested the entire conduct of the Club. The Committee so elected, shall proceed to the selection of a sub-committee, of seven of the general Committee to be then submitted and confirmed by the general meeting . . . That the sub-committee shall meet every Saturday at 2 o'clock . . . that the entrance subscription shall be 10 gns and the annual subscription be 6 gns . . . that members be invited to present their duplicate dramatic works to the committee, towards forming a library.'

Finally, to emphasise the informal and gregarious nature of this new club, 'Mr Mills stated that the proposed dinners were to be at 5 pm and the Bill called at 6.30 and that Musical parties were contemplated on the evenings the Theatres were not open.'

Reading these early minutes covering the last weeks of 1831 and the early days of 1832, there is an impression of bustle and highly effective self-reliance, a compatible team working well together, as it does today, but not always during the years in between. Mr Beazley was persuaded to act as honorary architect 'alterations not to exceed £500'; 'a legal person shall take care the agreement [with the builder, Bucke] is so drawn up that neither the Club nor the Committee shall be responsible for any debts contracted by Mr Bucke'; 'Mr Braham recommended a cook'; 'Mr Robins, Mr Durrant and Mr Beazley met at 2 o'clock and adjourned at 3 to Probatt's Hotel, where Sir Andrew Barnard joined. The assignment of the lease and furniture was executed by Mr George Robins and Mr Richard Williams, two of the Trustees, and a check given for £1,410'.

'Purchased for the coffee room: 3 mahogany tables 4' × 3', 11 mahogany tables 3' × 3', carpets, 4 window curtains, 48 chairs, standard light of 2 or 4 globes bronze . . .' and so on. And then, on the last day of November, 'that the seal or emblem of the club be a globe encircled with a ribband with the words "All the world's

a stage" and that two sketches be made thereof . . .'. 'Mr Mills and
Mr Jerdan visited Pellats Glass Manufactory, Black Friar's Bridge,
and chose the glass for the club.' 'Mr Smith [tradesman, not mem-
ber] provided wines – 597 bottles in the small wine cellar.'

By the middle of January, 1832, the cutlery had been polished,
the knives sharpened, the leather arm chairs installed in the smoking
room, fuel for the fires in the appropriate cellar, servants' uniforms
approved and purchased, Probatt's sign taken down and no other
erected in its place in customary club anonymity, the Duke of
Sussex as Patron had agreed to take the chair at the inaugural dinner,
tickets one guinea. At first it was to be on 1 February, but the smell
of paint led to its being postponed until Wednesday the 15th.

One hundred and ten members sat down at tables in the drawing
room and library. The Duke arrived at 7.05 pm, the Rev. Mr
Tallofield said grace, and after dinner the *Non Nobis* was sung before
toasts – the Duke giving The King, the national anthem following.
Toast: The Drama. Lord Mulgrave gave His Royal Highness the
Duke of Sussex, Captain Polhill gave success to Drury Lane Theatre,
Mr Kemble success to Covent Garden Theatre. The President of
the Club, and 'the unwearied promoters of its interests' were drunk;
then 'the Ladies, particularly those who adorn the Drama'.

For the inaugural dinner Barham even provided the lines for a
glee, put to music by the composer William Hawes, master of the
choristers at St Paul's Cathedral and the Chapel Royal. Between
them they could, it was felt even at the time, have done better. But
because it was an Occasion, and the title of this book requires
derivation, even if it has, so to speak, been promoted, it must be
quoted. But at the same time imagine the mellow state of the
hundred or so founder members present, the fumes of cigars in
the packed room, the flushed faces behind the sidewhiskers, and
the determination to make this an evening to remember:

> Let poets of superior parts
>   Consign to deathless fame
> The Larceny of the Knave of Hearts
>   Who spoiled his Royal Dame.

Alack! my timid muse would quail
Before such thievish cubs
But plumes a joyous wing to hail
Thy birth, fair QUEEN OF CLUBS.

Well, at least it was brief. At a later dinner to celebrate that evening the incorrigible Barham sang a song beginning 'Jove sat on Olympus, in glory array'd ...', and there followed five extremely long verses.

The Duke left at 11 pm, but the evening was by no means over. 'Lord William Lennox was called to the Chair, and several toasts, and songs, were given. The Company retired soon after Twelve, and all expressed themselves perfectly satisfied with the arrangements of the day.'

Within two years of the Club's establishment it was known that the Garrick was already collecting books, pictures and objects relevant to the theatre. Thus *The Observer* of 8 December 1833:

Independently of the recently large additions to the dramatic library of the Garrick Club a number of original theatrical portraits, etc., have been, within the last few months, presented to it by various members. Among them are the following: 1. A large picture, by Mather Brown, representing Pope, Mrs Pope, Mrs Wells, Hull, etc, in the last scene of *The Gamester*, given by M. Zachary, Esq. 2. An original brass bust of Garrick, done from the life by Roubilliac, cut in 1758, and for many years in the possession of Garrick, given by Peter Norton, Esq. 3. A bust of Shakespeare, given by G. Raymond, Esq. 4. A painting of Shakespeare (evidently an old picture, and at least as original as three-fourths of those included in Mr Boaden's book), given by H. Broadwood, Esq. 5. A set of engravings from well-known theatrical pictures, by Zoffany, given by W. Linley, Esq. 6. An admirable portrait of Mathews in the part of Monsieur Mallet, by Clint, given by Edward Parratt, Esq.

It is expected that Mathews, on his return to London, will make further additions from his theatrical gallery. The presents already made have been judiciously arranged in the library and drawing-rooms of the Club.

Charles Mathews was, indirectly, destined to provide more than that; he was to provide the heart of the Garrick collection of pictures two years later. (See Appendix A.)

35 King Street is generally described as 'cosy' and 'intimate' but never as commodious. A member would enter from the street by a double flight of stone steps into a gloomy hall in which was displayed the bust of Shakespeare, which adorns the Garrick hall today, and busts of a few celebrated actors. Turn left into the strangers' dining room, filling most of the ground floor, closely hung with pictures, like the present coffee room.

Next, along a dark passage to the smoking room, 'thought the most cheerful apartment in town' in the evenings. The coffee room 'devoted to members' dinners' was at the front up two flights of stairs, overlooking King Street. The morning room was behind, 'for newspapers and writing, and in which is the small but excellent library, rich in dramatic works',[7] together with the card room. There were apartments (no mention of how many) but no baths, of course; and the kitchens in the basement were 'very bad' even by the standards of the 1830s apparently, which possibly accounts for the high staff turnover.

There was, however, general contentment with the King Street premises, and meals, good, bad, and indifferent, continued to be cooked, throughout the 1830s, '40s and '50s. Conditions deteriorated during the 1850s, simply because of more members, the scale of discontent rising with the increase, from two hundred to three hundred, to four hundred. The trouble was that facilities could not be improved because of the confined space. For example, 'The Committee having considered the suggestions for establishing a Billiard Table and Baths, regret to state that these very desirable additions to the comforts of the Club are not immediately practicable.'[8] A complaint three years later, indirectly caused by overcrowding: 'Gentlemen, I venture to bring to your notice the extreme inconvenience which I in common with other members

of this Club suffer from the intolerable heat arising from the gas
in the small dining room.'⁹ It kept this member, and many others,
away from the place, the member complained to the Committee.

The smells, and the overcrowding, continued to increase. At
length, at a Committee meeting on 18 February 1860, Sir Charles
Taylor moved the following Resolution of which he had given
notice, when it was seconded and carried unanimously:

> That in the opinion of the Committee the Club House does not
> afford as much accommodation to Members as is desirable.
> That Mr Arden, Mr Dance and Sir Chas Taylor be appointed a
> sub-committee to enquire into the best means of rectifying such
> defect, and that these gentlemen be empowered to consult with
> proper persons, to have necessary plans and estimates made, and
> to enquire into the general financial position of the Club . . .

Just three months later, on 19 May 1860, the sub-committee
reported on 'the practicality of enlarging the house, and the general
financial condition of the Club'. The three members had certainly
worked speedily and diligently, reaching the conclusion that it was
both impractical and uneconomic to enlarge 35 King Street, and
that the best plan was to start from scratch on a site to be purchased,
as nearby as possible so as to remain in the hub of theatreland. A
lease should be purchased, the money to be raised as far as possible
by members themselves through debentures.

Copies of the report were despatched to every member, with a
notice that the resolution would be put to a Special General Meeting held on 9 June 1860. Ninety-one members turned up, and the
Saturday afternoon meeting, under the chairmanship of Lord
Tenterden, discussed this radical proposal for nearly two hours.
Members who quite properly regarded their club as a stable element
in their lives, and members who regarded a move of their own house
with relative equanimity, felt the chill draught of future unease
and discomfort. Many of those present, as founder members and
daily attenders, had used the Club for more than half their adult
lives; almost thirty years had passed since that first meeting at the
Drury Lane Theatre which had led to the Garrick's formation.

Doubts, misgivings and reservations were aired on that sultry afternoon, but when the vote was called for this resolution was carried unanimously, a reflection of the persuasive powers of Sir Charles Taylor:

> That, it having been found impracticable to increase the present building; the Committee be empowered to take such steps as they may deem advisable to secure a new and larger house. The thanks of the meeting were noted to the Chairman, and also to the sub-committee for their report . . .

From this meeting there was born a Building Committee which was 'empowered to issue debentures to the extent of £12,000 bearing interest at the rate of 5% per annum in order to raise the necessary funds for building a New Club House . . .' This figure, in the light of building costs, was later raised to £15,000.

The Building Committee kept in constant touch with the general committee, requesting, for example, on 1 February 1862, £500 'for the Purchase of Furniture for the New Club House'. By 5 April of that year £12,202 had been subscribed, which was now considered sufficient, and the list in the morning room was removed. Next, at a special meeting of the committee on 31 May: 'Mr Fladgate the *Solicitor*,' we read, 'submitted the engrossment of the deed of Trust, which requires three contributors Trustees to be appointed. Ordered that a letter be written to each of the contributors stating that a Special Meeting of the Club be summoned for the 23rd instant for the purpose of reading the Deed of Trust and obtaining the necessary signatures.' The three first Trustees were appointed at this meeting, there appears to have been no acrimony – they were all in it up to the neck by now – and thus by mid-summer 1862 the money was there, all properly accounted for, and the builders, having cleared away the rubble and detritus of ancient warehouses stinking of ancient fruit and vegetables, were bricklaying away only 200 yards from 35 King Street, and had already reached about half the final height of the building.

The design of the new building, 'in the Italian style', had been entrusted to the superintending architect to the Metropolitan Board of Works, Frederick Marrable, a judicious choice one would suppose.

It has a frontage of 96 feet to the street [runs a contemporary newspaper report] but the rear was very difficult, from its shape, to manage, and Mr Marrable has dealt very cleverly with the quaint form over which he had to lay out his chambers. The house is Italian, and is imposing, from having been judiciously and not over enriched. The entrance is by a recessed porch, not in the centre, but nearest west, so as to give the Club a splendid dining-room on the left, 49ft by 26ft. The smoking room (26ft by 32ft) is to the right, and in the rear are strangers' dining-rooms and smoking rooms, the former 34ft by 19ft, the latter 20ft by 17ft. In the hall is a very beautiful Italian screen. The noble staircase is of carved oak; at the top a landing-place of 26ft by 18ft. From this is entered the morning-room (35ft 6in by 26ft), the card-room (26ft by 23ft), and the library (27ft by 18ft). All the apartments demanded by the habits of the day – some of them were not thought necessary in the days of Garrick – are, of course, provided – two bath-rooms included. The hall and the corridor on the ground floor are paved with beautiful encaustic tiles, and the centre of the coffee-room is laid with parqueterie. The kitchens and all their arrangements are sumptuous, and the latest culinary improvements are introduced. The system of sunlights appears to be very complete, and devices for a perfect ventilation have not been forgotten. The contract for the work was taken at £9,880, and the entire expense, including the fittings, will be about £13,000. The invaluable pictures will not be immediately re-hung, but will be placed away until the last suspicion of any vestige of damp shall be dispelled.

The origin of the sobriquet 'the barn' for Mr Marrable's club house is lost in the mists of time. It just turns up every now and then and may not have been as widely used as the cartoon on page 68 suggests. Some members today call it 'the red barn', and the origin of that is quite clear and 'just a silly joke' as the member who coined it, the publisher Roland Gant, suggests. It appears that in turning down a lunch invitation because he had a table for an old wartime friend named Marten, and recalling the play first performed at the Marylebone on 6 April 1840, he gave as his excuse, 'I'm awfully sorry but I am already lunching Marten at the Red Barn.'

By 1864 the Garrick had become a very famous Club, and there was much curiosity about the new building and the move to take place in the summer. All the same, the move provoked a good deal of dissent and bad feeling. At the last minute a lot of members did not want to leave the cosy old place in King Street even if it did smell of gas, for the unfamiliar wide open spaces of the new building, especially those who had money tied up in 35 King Street and did not think they were getting a satisfactory deal over the sale. Others were nervous about the financial future for broader reasons, and because there would have to be a radical increase in numbers of members to support the rent. In May and June of 1864 there were critical and noisy meetings as the last weeks in King Street ran out.

On 7 May, with John Arden FSA in the chair, the Committee consisting of only Anthony Trollope, Wilkie Collins and Colonel de Bathe, it was decided that a General Meeting of the Club be called for Saturday 21 May at 3 pm to consider the resignation from the Club of three Committee members and no fewer than *twenty-four* ex-Committee members as well as two of the Club's Trustees, Sir Charles Taylor and Sir George Armytage. The points at issue were not only financial but the manner of handling the move and the move itself, even though the structure of the new building had been complete for some months. It is no surprise to find that the ballot for new members, to be taken at this meeting, was postponed for fourteen days 'in consequence of the unsettled state of the Club', although, goodness knows, they were likely to be urgently needed.

This fairly critical General Meeting was held at the New Club. The building was not yet ready for occupation but it was thought appropriate to signify that the old days were really over and this was, like it or not, the new home.

One hundred and fifty-eight members turned up to discuss all

these resignations including as well the threatened resignation of
the Club's debenture holders. It could hardly have been a worse
start, as the laconic minutes reveal, with Sir Charles Russell, age
33 (later Lord Russell of Killowen, Senior Trustee of the Club for
many years as well as Lord Chief Justice), 'objecting on the ground
that 14 days notice [of the motion] thereof had not previously been
given to the Secretary in accordance with Rule No. 3.'

The chairman overruled this objection, but the debenture holders and everyone else, having made the gesture, now suddenly
withdrew their resignations, amid (although it does not say so)
considerable uproar.

The full story, and the sums of money involved, are lost in the
mists of Covent Garden; but it *is* recorded that there was a meeting
of the sub-committee a week later back in King Street at which
Francis 'Papa' Fladgate read a letter: 'We the undersigned Debenture Holders deeply regret the proceedings which took place at the
recent General Meeting, convinced they are inconsistent with the
social interest, welfare and security of the Club.' Signed 'The
Debenture Holders, Garrick Club, 19 May, 1864.' This was noted,
and that was the last written reference to this row.

There was a last minute rush to complete the decorations, leading to the postponement by two weeks of the proposed anniversary
dinner to 'celebrate' the move. The Secretary was 'desired to effect
a further insurance of £7,000 on the new building', making
£12,000 in all. The last ever meeting in King Street took place on
2 July at which a proposal was passed, 'That on and after 4th July
inst this house be closed with the exception of the morning and
strangers rooms and that no cooked provisions shall be supplied'.

Like any domestic move, chaos and confusion prevailed during
these final days. There is a note of near-hysteria in the resolution
(16 July), 'The decoration of the Members' Smoking Room was
ordered to be proceeded with at once.' John Arden undertook to
superintend this urgent work and also to supervise the removal of
the contents of the library and the strangers' dining room, and all
the pictures. Then, the end of an era: 'It was ordered that on and
after Monday next the 5th day of September 1864 the Club House

be closed and the gas put out in all the public rooms at 2 a.m.
precisely'.

So that was that, and things would never be the same again. They
would not indeed. On that same day the cook was sacked, and a
new one had to be found – salary £160–£180 pa. By December
it was clear that the finances were already precarious; and it was
proposed to enlarge the number of members to 600. Nobody even
knew the club's address now. What did you say to a cabby when
you wanted to get there? When the new street had been carved
through the squalid tenements and alleyways of Covent Garden,
the Committee wanted it to be called Shakespeare Street. Members
did not object to that, whatever else they were grumbling about.
But the Metropolitan Board of Works did. They wanted to call it
New King Street, and so it was, briefly. But on the grounds that
the building completely dominated the immediate surroundings,
the Committee countered with Garrick Street; and the M.B.W.
at length agreed, persuaded perhaps by the ubiquitous Mr Marrable.

And here, in Garrick Street, the roots of the Club have grown and
strengthened like an oak – incidentally, a sapling planted in the
back yard in 1864 would at the time of writing comfortably brush
the billiard room windows on the top floor. The only crises to put
the Club's venue at risk have been financial, although there was a
suggestion in 1904 that the premises should be moved out of
theatreland into the traditional clubland calm of St James's.

As usual, some 'penny-a-liner' leaked the news to the press, and
the outcome. On 20 July 1904 the *Daily Chronicle* carried this story:

By a considerable majority the members of the Garrick Club
have decided not to migrate to St James's-square. A Committee
was appointed to consider the question, and presented two
reports. The minority report was adverse to migration, and at a
special meeting of the Club this was adopted, mainly on account
of the financial argument. In its historic haunt the Garrick pays

a modest rental of less than £300 a year; but in St James's-square it would have to pay £60,000 for a freehold. Some members think its situation is now too easterly for social convenience; and they find the walk through Leicester square depressing, although the statue of Shakespeare does all it can to cheer them. Still, the Club is flourishing, if not so sprightly as of yore.

The original lease of the land was for eighty years, and in 1925, with only seventeen years to run, the Trustees wisely decided that every effort should be made to secure the freehold of the premises, something they had been trying to do for several years. At the A.G.M. that year a long and comprehensive resolution was put to members, pointing out the dangers of letting the lease expire. 'The rent the Club is now paying is £289 per annum, and the net assessment of the Club for rateable purposes is £1,127 per annum. The price the freeholders are asking for the freehold is £23,000 and it is obvious that as the lease runs out the value of the freehold will become larger.'

The Committee did not consider the asking price as exorbitant, and, the resolution assured members, this sum could be borrowed from an insurance company at the rate of $5\frac{1}{4}\%$ per annum. It was proposed, in fact, to take out a mortgage for £30,000. The reason for this sounds strange today and reflects the contemporary casual attitude towards payment of tradesmen. 'For many years the Club has been run on credit,' the resolution continued. 'There has been an overdraft at the Bank, and considerable sums have been owing to tradesmen for long periods. In the past it has always been necessary to devote the whole of the current year's subscriptions in paying the previous year's bills to tradesmen ... The result has been that interest on the overdraft has had to be paid and it has been impossible to deal with our Suppliers on the best terms.'

There was much more besides, but the burden of this close-printed two-page resolution was that members' subscriptions would rise from 13 guineas to 15 guineas in order to accomplish this purchase 'for the benefit of their Successors'.

The historic resolution was passed. The Club became the property of its members; and the insecurity of a lease was exchanged for the burden of a mortgage – now happily at last paid off. Except for the ludicrous recent attempt by the government to get the Garrick out of Mr Marrable's 'red barn' (see p. 53) there has been no serious disturbance in members' tenure since that frenzied and fretful inauguration on 4 July 1864.

Recently the Garrick's West Room, originally Smoking Room, that large and rather awkward strangers' dining room on the ground floor looking on to Garrick Street, has been renamed the A. A. Milne Room, for a very good reason described elsewhere. And the few last surviving card players have been crammed into a part of the old office on the first floor. But over more than 120 years there have been few internal alterations or even changes of usage within the club, except in the staff, kitchen and storage quarters. Some older members recall when they were young hearing from very old members that the billiards table was originally on the first floor, occupying the present reading room. Downstairs the staff have been provided with quarters more appropriate to the 1980s than the 1860s, food stores and cooking facilities could not elicit the trace of a raised eyebrow from the scrutiny of outside inspectors; and passing pedestrians in Garrick Street tread unknowingly over extended cellars housing vineyards of maturing claret and burgundy.

Some fourteen years after the bar began business in what is now the reading room, the press of numbers and the noise level forced it into its present more spacious quarters, and later a second entry was knocked through into the ex-bar so that up to four members at a time could enter the bar at peak times before lunch, and in swift succession. A flat has been provided for the secretary, there is a natty new bathroom next to the billiards room on the top floor. Amongst the hard core of billiards and snooker players there is much complaining of this inaccessibility – seventy stairs excluding the front steps.

[29]

Most proposed changes have caused outrage; almost all alterations actually carried out even worse outrage. A lift has been proposed a dozen or more times; on the first occasion the estimate was about £300; the most recent £60,000.

The small lounge in the well of the stairs has been a source of intermittent controversy both as to usage and its ludicrously unsuitable location. It is the natural and most convenient place for guests to settle down to await their delayed member-host, and for lady guests to rest their weary legs while their host pays the bill or is otherwise temporarily occupied elsewhere. It is not comfortable to evict gentlemen strangers, and highly embarrassing to ask women to leave what appears to be – and is – really a more comfortable extension of the hall. Be all that as it may, it has been exclusive to members for many years, and judging by the violent reaction to any suggested change, will remain so for ever.

Even the creation of this anachronism was a matter of club controversy. Before 1902 it was part of a spacious hall extending to under the staircase, where members and their guests – male of course – greeted one another and gossiped or exchanged a last blurred word before leaving. Then the sub-committee thought it would be a nice place to sit down with a drink and a cigar, chat, and watch the Garrick world go by; which is exactly what is so pleasant about it today, noting who is arriving for lunch or dinner, the new suit he may be wearing (and how it fits), the apparent state of their health, and whether old Judge Partridge's limp is even worse.

But 'Dear Sir,' wrote the barrister from Old Square, Charles Sweet, to the secretary C. J. Fitch, on 23 July 1902, 'I beg to enclose a protest, signed by twenty members of the Club, against the proposed conversion of the hall into a smoking lounge. The matter has come upon the Club very unexpectedly, and many of the members are out of town, otherwise the number of signatures would have been much larger . . .' – a typical advocate's speculative assumption. 'I shall be obliged by your laying the protest before the sub-committee at the earliest possible moment.' A couple of days later he gathered another dozen signatures, but all to no avail.

At the time of writing, readers will note with relief, no further changes of name or usage of any part of the Club are contemplated; and the Garrick ' 'mid all revolution in the hopes and fears of men, doth still remain unchanged'; just as Sean O'Casey found it: 'A pile of stone, mortar, and bricks that told a visitor nothing.'[10]

2

Committees

'The number of the members is limited and the character of the Club is social and therefore the electing Committee is compelled to exercise a very vigilant care for it is clear that it would be better that ten unobjectionable men should be excluded than that one terrible bore should be admitted.'
JOHN TIMBS on The Garrick, 1872.

THE SENTIMENT ABOVE is unobjectionable, too. But there is a vocal school of thought at the Garrick that believes a bore is an essential element in the structure of a good club: as a butt, as a joke, as the progenitor of appalling tales of avoidance and enmeshment. As a village needs an idiot, a Cabinet a leak-er, a lêvée a faux pas, so a good club needs a bore, if only to highlight the contrast with the boring outside world.

The minutes of the Garrick Club's Committees record not just the election or blackballing of candidates for membership, bores and non-bores, but cast a (usually discreet) eye over the month-to-month life of the club, routine and exceptional, making and amending rules, occasionally bending them, reflecting the mood and opinions of the Club. These minutes are contained in numerous bound volumes, latterly typewritten, thank goodness, but for the most part handwritten by the current secretary or *his* secretary and mostly in copper-plate, with a few riotous breaks into the near-indecipherable, caused either by drink or a stand-in. From time to time the march of history is echoed, like the death of a monarch or a war, or economic slumps and their regretted resignations and frantic searches to find new members with their entrance fees and subscriptions.

The King Street minutes are brief, fairly uninformative and mainly indecipherable, brown ink fading into greying paper. A sampling of Committee meeting minutes of the pre-Garrick Street period hints at a much smaller community, with a cramped club house and around 350 to 400 members. This neanderthal period appears to have been more convivial and less acrimonious than the Victorian years in Garrick Street, in spite of Thackeray-Yates-Dickens and other explosions of wrath (see p. 117). The meeting in April 1858 was above average in interest.

Minutes of the Committee
Saturday 3rd April 1858
Present
Lord Tenterden in the Chair

Lord Wm Lennox	Mr Thackeray
Sir C. Taylor	Mr Ovey
Mr Welch	Mr Harley
Mr Arnold	Mr Cunningham
Mr Fladgate	Mr Arabin
Mr Dickens	Col de Bathe

Read and confirmed the Minutes of the last Meeting of the Committee.

Ordered that cheques be drawn to pay the following bills: [There follows a long list, including Baker £5.16s, Fish £12.9s.6d., Ward (wine) £23.16s.6d, soda water £12.14s.6d, gin £7, Wages £51.2s]

Read the following letter from Mr Charles Kean:

> Sir,
>
> It will afford me very great pleasure to comply with the flattering request of the Garrick Committee to preside at the Annual Dinner on Friday 23rd April. The only possible impediment to my doing so, would arise from the play of *King Lear* not being ready for production on Saturday 17th April as at present arranged. I do not in the slightest degree apprehend such a result, but at the same time I wish to guard against any unfortunate circumstance.
>
> I am, sir, your obedient servt.
>
> Charles Kean

[33]

Read the following requisition signed by 31 members:

> The Shakespeare Dinner
> The Committee are requested to reconsider the subject of the above dinner, with a view to ascertaining, whether, if even at the risk of some extra trouble, it cannot take place, as formally *in the Club*.
>
> Much of its *agreeable prestige* being lost, by a change in *locale* in the opinion of the following members:

Ordered that a Copy of the following notice be placed in the Coffee Room:

> The Committee in reply to the requisition this day laid before them, have to inform those members who have signed it:
> That the Annual Dinner was removed from the Club last year very much against the inclination of the Committee, but that they considered the change forced upon them (after careful enquiry) by the great increase in the number of members, and the absolute impossibility of continuing to hold the dinner in any one of the Club Rooms, with due regard to the general comfort and convenience. These reasons existing in greater force this year, the Committee even if they had made no contract with the Albion [hotel] would have been wholly unable to comply with the request preferred to them.

Read letter from Sir Charles Ibbetson.

The Secretary reported the following gentlemen as not having paid their subscription for the current year:

> Earl of Cottenham
> Mr James Davidson
> Captain J. Evelyn
> Mr Kenneth Macaulay

Ordered that Lord Cottenham's name be erased from the list of members, and that Mr James Davidson, Captain Evelyn and Mr

Kenneth Macaulay be written to and allowed a fortnight longer for the payment of their subscriptions, and that in future the Article 19 of the Rules and Regulations of the Club be enforced. Sir Charles Taylor gave notice that he should move at the next meeting of the Committee 1stly That a copy of the following notice be entered in the minute book of the Club, & 2ndly that a copy be also placed in the Coffee Room.

The attention of the Committee having been called to the fact that allusions to what has passed in the Garrick Club, to the conduct of its members, and to the management of its affairs have lately appeared in the columns of certain newspapers, they wish hereby to put on record their opinion that the writers of such paragraphs are in any case guilty of doing what must give offence to the Members of this Society, & further, were it possible to imagine those writers to be Members of the Garrick Club, they would be culpable of a most serious transgression of the laws which regulate the social intercourse of gentlemen.

Lord de Lennox gave notice that he should move at the next meeting of the Committee – 'That the list of Members on the ballotting list shall be extended to double the number of those members actually to be ballotted for, in order that should the full number on the list not be elected by the first names in rotation, the same number of vacancies may be filled up by the succeeding names.'

The following candidates were elected:

Honble. Percy Fielding and the Honble W. Fielding
Colonel de Bathe was selected by the Chairman to ascertain with him the result of the Ballot, Lord Wm Lennox, Sir C. Taylor, Mr C. Dickens, Mr Thackeray & Mr Arabin inspected the Ballot boxes.
Ordered that the next six names be placed on the list for Ballot at the next meeting.

(signed) Tenterden

The fifty years or so after the members had settled into their new premises in 1864 reflect the pax Britannica beyond the soot-stained walls, and the current convention of restraint and discretion. *Nothing* seems to happen beyond the purchase of 150 pints of Moët, a change of butcher, a replacement of staff, the regret at the death of some old stalwart who could remember the day Charles Dickens came to lunch for the first time, the election of his replacement from the world outside, a mild protest at a member bringing a guest into the smoking room at the wrong time, a decision to buy a second copy of the *Pall Mall Gazette*. In short, the records are as reticent and dull as the life of a junior clerk on the Metropolitan Line. The following minutes are relatively lively:

> *At a* meeting of the *General* Committee
> *Held* Saturday *Jan: 13* 1900 at 3½ o'clock
> *Present:*– J. C. O'Dowd Esq *Chair*, W. L. Courtney, C. T. Gill Q C, H. E. Gurner Esqres, Gen. Lambton, E. H. Martineau, C. W. Mathews, A. N. Piner Esq, Sir H. B. Poland, M. B. Praed Esq, Col: Segrave, Sir D. Straight, H. D. Traill Esq, Sir C. Rivers Wilson
> *Minutes* of meeting held April 29 1899 read and confirmed.
> Read *letter* from Sir Squire Bancroft offering for acceptance accompanying portrait of Garrick (attributed to Zoffany) and painted for his friend Hannah More. Accepted and unanimously agreed to offer the Committee's cordial and hearty role of thanks for the gift.
> Read list of *Deaths*, *Withdrawals*, during 1899, Deaths 16, Resignations 13, Other causes 1, Total 30, Secretary pointing out that in this list was included the name of the Duke of Beaufort, Trustee.
> At a *ballot* held the following gentlemen were elected members of the Club:
>
> | | |
> |---|---|
> | Edward Wagg | Bulkeley C. Praed |
> | John Kemp | Anthony White★ |
> | | (subsequently declined to take up his election) |

Things get more interesting and eventful, naturally enough, with the arrival of the Kaiser's war. Following the first Zeppelin raid on

London on 1 June 1915, 'the question of reviewing the insurance against damage by air-craft' was discussed. And, after the Gallipoli fiasco and more butchery in Flanders, a Roll of Honour, it was proposed, should be displayed. A major who was killed before he could use the Club should have his entrance fee and first year's subscription refunded to his family, Sir Charles Mathews proposed.[2]

The war-to-end-war's chronology is reflected in the club's record. As food becomes scarce a 3s 6d set dinner is introduced,[3] and with emergency legislation to save fuel, guests are allowed into the morning room after 7 pm.[4] When it later becomes necessary to halve the consumption of electricity, the supply of toast with paté is discontinued and the billiards room is 'partially closed'.[5] In the last months of the Great War even *bread* with paté is slashed from the menu, and the guest charge is increased to discourage their presence.[6] Perhaps more serious, Sir Charles Jessel, Chairman of the Imperial Continental Gas Association, 'called attention to the vastly increased consumption of liquors in the Club and to the practical impossibility of renewing the stocks'.[7] The problem was swiftly and not surprisingly solved.

But on the whole, Garrick life proceeded on its customary domestic course. Members were allowed to take guests to the billiards room (when open);[8] it was decided that when 12 committee members were present, two blackballs would exclude a candidate for membership; more than 12, three blackballs.[9] Lord Burnham, who had just lost his father (proprietor of the *Daily Telegraph*) was elected a member of the Committee, so was Gerald du Maurier, Sir John Hare, lately manager of the Garrick Theatre, H. A. Vachell, the popular novelist, and Edward Marshall Hall, one of the most famous advocates of the time. To their relief, there were no blackballs at their first meeting.[10]

Sir Francis Burnand, a member since 1865 and editor of *Punch* for almost as long, was elected an honorary member in February 1916; 'a gift by Lady Tree of a silver salver given to H. M. Tree by Queen Victoria in 1894 was accepted with thanks'.[11] Alfred Duff Cooper was elected a member in February 1918 before he marched off to the war – 'The band played nearly all the way,' he wrote to his wife Diana. 'I felt proud, romantic and exalted.'[12] And no wonder, because he was leading his draft to Waterloo Station, the officer deputed to do so being too drunk.

Two notable bookmen were elected at the same meeting, Daniel Macmillan and E. V. Lucas, along with Freddy Lonsdale (*The Last of Mrs Cheyney*) and Henry's grandson, the artist Laurence Irving, only twenty years old but viewed sympathetically because his father had been drowned after a U-boat attack on the ship in which he was a passenger.[13] Today, happily, he is our oldest member, a life member, and our most senior member.

In the closing stages of the war, Mrs Lockett Agnew wrote to Mr N. Forbes-Robertson 'offering to the Club a portrait of David Garrick by Peni in accordance with the wishes of her late husband'.[14] This was accepted by the Committee at almost the last meeting with Charles Fitch as Club Secretary. In May 1919, with the younger members who had survived back to a land fit for heroes, and the Garrick, the new Secretary Lieut-Colonel C. O. Greenwell OBE was made an honorary member and given a salary of £400 p.a. One of his first duties was to report to the Committee the death at the early age of forty-nine of Henry Irving, the great actor's younger son and Laurence's uncle, who had made his own first appearance on the professional stage under Hare in 1891. A letter of condolence and flowers were sent to his widow, Dorothea, who had made her first outstanding success (as Dorothea Baird) in the name part in *Trilby* in 1895. 'Will you convey to the Committee of the Garrick Club,' she wrote (28 October 1919) 'my heartfelt thanks for the beautiful flowers they sent in my dear husband's memory'.

The misery of a burglary of silver and the defacement of a page of the candidates' book (neither for the last time, alas) was offset by the acceptance by the Prince of Wales of Honorary Membership in May 1921. Less than a year later a member 'laid before the Committee his proposal for the introduction of Ladies to the Club for luncheon, tea and dinner'. Thus began, in the flood tide of post-war women's emancipation (now they even had the *vote*, if they were over twenty-nine), the Garrick Club's own private internal war, still rumbling on today, in which the forces of established misoneism – the misognynists – have fought a slow, implacable rearguard action against revisionists, particularly from artists, in this case Rowland Berkeley. Ten years later, for example, women might be found dining in the private rooms, but a suggestion that they might be shown round the premises to examine the pictures was thrown out instantly; and a proposal that ladies might be permitted to take luncheon in the coffee room on Sundays got equally short shrift.

That was in 1931, an eventful year for the club, which lost Arnold Bennett through his death and gained Cedric Hardwicke on behalf of drama, Melford Stevenson on behalf of the law and K. S. Duleepsinhji on behalf of India and cricket. It was the Club's centenary, and in spite of the grave national financial crisis the Garrick determined to put on a show. A slap-up dinner at the Savoy Hotel, it was proposed at the 4 June meeting, would meet the case and also allow all members to attend, the coffee room being unable to accommodate more than 100. And why not ask H. R. H. The Prince of Wales, just as an ordinary member, to sit where he likes, and 'not make a speech unless so minded'. 4 or 11 October?

That idea was knocked on the head when H. R. H. said he wanted to come to the *Garrick* if it was a Garrick occasion, not some hotel, which made very good sense. Admiral Sir Lionel Halsey, Comptroller and Treasurer (Battles of Ladysmith, Heligoland Bight, Dogger Bank and Jutland), would suggest dates in due course. (22 November was the final choice.)

The club secretary, J. W. Wharton, and the steward, S. Sandell, showed an independent line of celebration, however, by absconding with £1,100, a large sum of money in 1930 – say £15,000 in 1985. The first news of this scandal was reported by Lord Buckmaster to the Committee on 4 December 1930, after one of those desperate efforts, reported from time to time, to change the club tie. Then two resolutions were put forward:

Resolution proposed by Sir Charles Biron and seconded by Sir Dunbar Plunket Bart. was passed: 'That Sandell having been

guilty of misconduct, should, in accordance with Rule 9 of the
Staff Provident Fund Rules, forfeit all his share of the Staff
Provident Fund except such portion as he had contributed
himself.'

The following Resolution proposed by Sir Chartres Biron and
seconded by Mr A. de C. Parmiter was passed: 'That Mr Wharton,
the late Secretary, having been dismissed for misconduct involv-
ing dishonesty and fraud, should, in accordance with Rule 10
of the Staff Provident Fund Rules, forfeit all moneys standing
to his credit in the Staff Provident Fund, and that such moneys
should be absorbed in the General Account of the Fund.'

Later 'a detailed account of the defalcations' was given at a
Special General Meeting. Half the money was recovered from the
insurance company, but only after the usual tussle, and legal proceedings were taken against the auditors. Considerable care was
taken over the appointment, and only six months' trial to start
with, of a successor. The gallant Lieutenant-Colonel Kenneth
Plimpton DSO was appointed from 1 April 1931 at £650 pa, £200
more than his unfortunate predecessor, plus food. Plimpton's first
request was that if he ceased to be the secretary of the club 'through
no discreditable reason' he would be allowed to rejoin as an ordinary
member. This was agreed without discussion. He arrived at a difficult as well as an eventful period, including all the arrangements
for the centenary dinner, went on to serve the club through the
1930s and the Hitler war, giving way to Lieut-Colonel S.E.L.
Baddeley, 'a firm, just man,' according to one of the waitresses
today who worked under his command when she was just nineteen.
    The proceedings were concluded by a major injection of literary
talent into the club: Peter Fleming, Edgar Wallace, Francis Brett
Young, Rupert Hart-Davis, Ivor Brown and Gerald Gould were
all elected.
    The finances were awful in 1930, worse still in 1931. The three
trustees, Lord Buckmaster, Lord Burnham and Sir Arthur Pinero,
began to fear the worst might happen. Members resigned through
penury, or simply died and were not replaced in sufficient numbers,

the overheads remaining the same for fewer members. As before, and since, the crisis was resolved by one or two business members, usually despised by actors when they are not saving the club: in this case Geoffrey Russell and Howard Dunkley.

Centenary year was rounded off by the presentation by that long-time stalwart of the club, Sir Francis Fladgate, son of 'Papa', of a complete run of the *Spectator*, from Nos 1 to 78, once the property of David Garrick.

Literature again figured heavily in the first weeks of 1932, beginning with the election of the agreeable Beverley Nichols, with the light touch, and the not-so-cheerful (*The Shape of Things to Come*) H.G.Wells; to be offset later in the year by the death of Kenneth Grahame. Then there was the luncheon party of J.B. Priestley and his publisher, Charlie Evans of Heinemann. At the meeting on 7 January 1932, the Chairman, seconded by Arthur Pinero, proposed that a letter be sent to these two literary members 'asking if they could give any information or comment on a notice in *The Times* of 30 December 1931 of a lunch they gave . . .' The cutting was passed round the table with a lot of tut-tutting: 'A luncheon party,' it read, 'was held at the Garrick Club yesterday to meet the American author Mr Charles Norris. The hosts were Mr J.B.Priestley and Mr Norris's publisher Mr C.S.Evans. The guests included Mr J.C.Squire, Mr Victor Gollancz, Mr Robert Lynd, Mr Arthur Bliss, Mr Ivor Brown, Mr Ralph Straus and Mr Gerald Gould.' Not only was it considered unseemly to 'advertise' the Garrick Club in this way; but the list of guests – most of them literary editors – underlined the fact that this was a *business luncheon*. Oh dear! The members apologised profoundly and the apology was accepted formally at the next meeting.

For most clubs, blackballing comes in waves, and like an orgy, is succeeded by remorse and a determination to lead a purer life. However justified the blackballing may be – and it nearly always is – the atmosphere in the Committee, and in the bar afterwards, is compounded of a strange mixture of elation, sanctimoniousness and guilt. There is nothing quite like it, except perhaps the aftermath of killing people, in war I hasten to add.

[41]

Be that as it may, there was a wave of blackballing in 1933, a time when new members and their entrance money and subscriptions were desperately needed. But Leslie Howard was in and so was the novelist's grandson, James Makepeace Thackeray. This blackballing was followed as always by many post mortems and earnest resolutions to reform. At the meeting on 15 February 1934: 'The committee shall at the meeting prior to the meeting arranged for the election of Candidates consider the names of those who have been duly nominated, and at this meeting the Chairman shall invite each Member individually to express his opinion.' One hopes members got at least the burden of this appalling legalese. Also: 'It shall be an understanding that any member of the Committee who intends to oppose the election of a Candidate shall make a confidential communication to the Chairman of the Sub-Committee.' No stabs in the back, please. These resolutions were passed, there were fewer blackballs, but, like broken treaties with all their cost and anguish, the rules were soon circumvented or fell into disuse.

Sir Gerald du Maurier, whose father had hung up his trilby for the last time in the Garrick in 1896, died on 11 April 1934, and his passing was noted and regretted.

Money still being tight that year, the installation of new fireplaces was postponed but as the rewiring of the club had become *urgently* necessary, this was carried out at a cost of £1,000, and improved ventilation for the coffee room went ahead, requiring the closing of the club for *one day* – those were the days.

Financial matters further improved, as it did almost everywhere, as rearmament got under way. The Club mortgage was reduced from 5% to 4½%, which allowed table money at lunch to be reduced by 3d per head. The staff benefited, too, not from rearmament but the deaths in 1934 of Lord Buckmaster, Sir Nigel Playfair and Sir Arthur Pinero, all of whom left bequests to the Staff Fund. Pinero also left a bust of himself, and, more meaningfully, all his future royalties. For many years these royalties were of enormous importance to the Club's finances – £4,000 to £5,000 a year when pounds were pounds.

The Pinero factor was not reflected at once, though, and the finances took another knock in 1936, with revenue down £1,000, due, it was explained, to a falling off in entrance fees; but, one suspects, more because of mismanagement. 1936 also saw the death of George V, the accession of Edward VIII, who after 14 years of 'ordinary membership', agreed to become Patron – 'graciously pleased to grant his patronage' wrote Lord Wigram, Keeper of the King's Purse, who should have been co-opted as an extra Trustee. Probably there was no connection between the 'clearing the Club of rats' (£30) and the advent of the new Royal Patron.

The Annual Club Dinner, long in abeyance, was reintroduced in 1937. It was a great success. There was a revival of some of the Club's old spirit in the months before the outbreak of world war again, as there had been in 1912–14. The idea of a dinner for Allan Aynesworth and Sir Seymour Hicks to celebrate their stage jubilee on 30 January 1938 was put forward at the meeting on 2 December.

On 3 March 1938 the question of a cocktail bar, in the strangers' smoking room, was raised, and referred to the sub-committee (soon to be renamed house committee). The sub-committee (amazingly) said yes, and that £100 should be appropriated for this purpose, a sum, they rightly reckoned, which would be made up within days of its opening in extra revenue. All the same, they remarked cautiously, the matter was of such fundamental importance that it should be put to the Annual General Meeting.

At the A.G.M. one alert member recalled that the question of a bar had been brought up for the first time on 6 April 1933 – and although the member did not say so, it can safely be assumed that the proposal was met with a sharp intake of members' breath. It was certainly rejected. In this more enlightened time, the matter was at least debated, although no one then, or later, seemed to realize that in King Street at the beginning there had been both a bar and a barmaid. Sir Charles Biron (Eton, Trinity Cambridge, the Bar 1886 and co-author of *On Extradition*) was the chief cause of the proposal being thrown out after speaking 'at some length'. We can only imagine the tedium, especially as everyone had already made up their minds. Three members, however, feeling like characters in an H.M.Bateman drawing, voted in favour.

In October 1938 a Fleet Street member, Mr James Douglas, age seventy-one, was roundly rebuked for exposing the Club in an article in the *Sunday Express* of 2 October:

> As we sat together on Wednesday at lunch in the Garrick Club peace was at its last gasp. Its death rattle sounded in our ears. All round us grave men were past hoping. Despair froze every heart.
>
> Ian Hay had come from a rehearsal of his new play. He had fixed Tuesday for its production. He had postponed it, because the jittered company could not learn their lines. The only two members of the cast who had learned their lines were boys!
>
> 'Don't postpone your play,' I said. 'There will be peace before Tuesday.' He shook his war-worn old head. He could not share my faith in peace. Nobody believed me.
>
> I stood up in the famous lounge and proclaimed my certitude. Derision was my portion! But in three hours the House of Commons was cheering and Queen Mary was weeping with joy.

The Committee 'would be glad of an assurance from him that such an incident would not occur again'.

With the increasing likelihood of another war with Germany the Garrick, like every institution in London, considered urgent precautions against bombing. On 17 April, 1939, the Picture Committee for the first time talked in strictly practical terms: what to do with the pictures. It resulted in 212 of the most valuable pictures being removed, without their glass, to a mansion 'near Newport Pagnall'. For many months, until cheap prints were brought to fill the empty frames, the walls of the Garrick looked like the aftermath of a burglars' raid instead of an air raid.

The first wartime Committee meetings were like a re-run of the proceedings in 1914. What about the subscription of those members joining their regiment or volunteering for the colours? Or members whose offices were evacuated to the country? On 5 October it was decided that there would be no reduction in subscription – that could bankrupt the place overnight. However, members could choose instead to resign, and 'those wishing to rejoin at a later date would be considerately dealt with'. There were later variations on this ruling, too frequent and complicated to go into. But the Club was to be closed on Sundays, and at 11 pm on weekdays, though this was rescinded on 7 December as the phoniness of the war deepened.

The 108th A.G.M. was held on 29 April 1940, twenty days after the invasion of Norway and with only twenty members present. The chairman warned of likely financial losses and pleaded with those present to find some new members. Lord Jessel suggested the introduction of paper table napkins. At the following ordinary meeting in May the shortage of members was again discussed and it was decided that the payment of the entrance fee could be spread over the year. But Mr W. Brown, a club servant for more than twenty years, was granted his £172 0s 10d from the Staff Fund on retirement, and also given a £2 per week pension.

The Committee in the early years of the war consisted of Lord Russell, in the chair, Allan Aynesworth, A. E. W. Mason, Bronson Albery, Major G. C. S. Black, Ralph Gore, Lt-Colonel C. P. Hawkes, Sir Travers Humpreys, the Hon. Edward H. Jessel, Roland Pertwee, Reginald Poole, G. C. Rivington and R. S. Turnbull. On 2 January 1941 a wartime subscription of 3 guineas was introduced, and the publisher, A. Dwye Evans, Charlie Evans's son, was the first to apply for this concession.

The bombing was an inconvenience and led to a drop in attendance, especially in the evenings, and to several windows being blown out, in spite of the regulation tape criss-crossing. From time to time there was no gas or electricity, but as the Committee proudly boasted, 'There was not a day when luncheons were not served'. A letter was sent to the Westminster City Council asking for steps to be taken to protect the statue of Henry Irving in Charing Cross Road. The Council complied, and that notable actor and member disappeared behind bricks for the duration.

At the 1941 A.G.M. the Chairman of the House Committee, Mr Rivington, recounted that there had been a drop in subscription revenue (and no wonder) of £1,063 and a reduction in revenue from provisions of £383, wines £400 and cigars £33. But strict economies in repairs, newspapers, laundry, etc had led to a saving of £1,380, leading to an overall loss of only £65.

Three days before Pearl Harbor the American Embassy was invited to forward the names of twelve Americans for honorary membership during their term of office in London. On the other hand an approach from members of the Empire Societies War Hospital Committee for honorary Club membership was turned down – 'no room'.

'For the duration' war measures included permitting guests in the lounge after 2 pm and ladies to take lunch at the side tables in the coffee room on Sundays, a privilege that was never rescinded – the thin end of the wedge indeed.

The musical element in the Club was greatly strengthened by the election of Arthur Bliss and William Walton (November 1942) and Ivor Newton in January 1943. Kenneth Horne cheered the place up at the same time, but Flight-Lieutenant Richard Hillary, recovered from his terrible burns in the Battle of Britain, was killed flying on the night he was elected.

The Pinero bequest yielded a bonanza of £8,000, of which – after a lot of discussion – £5,000 was used to help pay off the mortgage, £2,000 went into government securities and £1,000 was put aside for the purchase of wine, when it could be bought. In tune with the grim times – early 1943 – the Club was closed at 10 pm, when members desperately competed with American servicemen for taxis or groped their way home through the blackout. London was heavily bombed again with the result, on a prosaic note, that the Electricity Supply Company, which had set up a noisy piece of machinery adjacent to the rear of the Club many years before and had paid the useful compensation of £112 p.a., ceased payment. In the Club's closest shave of the war, a bomb had destroyed the source of the noise.

In the floodtide of wartime elections, many new members appeared, some of them happily still alive, who were to make a special mark on the club, like David Farrer, Alistair Sim and Michael Redgrave, Robert Henriques and Hugh Sinclair, Nicolas Bentley of the fine pen line, all of late lamented memory, John

Clements and Raymond Huntley of stage and screen, Arthur Ransome ('fanatical fisherman' and *Swallows and Amazons*), the historian John Ehrman, a 23-year-old sailor then, and John Gloag, Sir Kenneth Clark and Christopher Chancellor, all made their entrance.

With the entrance fee down to just one guinea, no wonder there was such a clamour to join. This led, naturally enough, to a drastic reduction in revenue from this source, and a great deal of acrimony when there was another orgy of blackballing in the summer of 1944 – though Terence Rattigan got through all right, just. As night follows day, another post-mortem took place. The sub-committee responsible at that time for putting names forward for election, was asked 'to make a general survey of the present method of election of candidates' and report later. It did: '. . . that any member of the Committee who feels doubtful about the suitability of a candidate shall make a confidential communication to the chairman of the sub-committee'.

In the outside world, France was liberated, and a minor and unofficial part of the celebrations led to a proposal in Paris to set up a 'Garrick Club de France'. A few Committee members were rather touched and flattered when this news was read out from a letter from Charles Morgan; but, *hélas*, a majority objected. The entrance fee was put up to 20 guineas, Henry Irving was 'unbricked', the pictures were brought back from their 'mansion near Newport Pagnall', Sir Thomas Beecham failed yet again to pay his bill: peace had returned, and with it a new secretary.

Colonel Plimpton resigned on 1 November 1945, with a £200 p.a. pension. Lieut-Colonel S. E. L. Baddeley then took over the reigns of command, and responsibility for Sir Thomas Beecham's unpaid bill; it took solicitors' letters and another four months to get *that* settled.

At the 1946 A.G.M. the new secretary was able to proclaim with justifiable pride that 22,587 meals had been served in the previous year, 2,745 more than in 1939, when there was no rationing. Reciprocal arrangements with two New York clubs, the Players and Century, which has led to much mutual satisfaction, convenience and joyful exchange (in every sense) ever since, were set up respectively in July 1946 and January 1947. This allowed a special telegram of congratulation to be sent to the Century for their centenary a few days later.

Another landmark: from 3 October 1946 ladies were allowed to use the morning room on Sundays up to 3 pm.

2 October 1947: 'It having been ascertained that Lieutenant Philip Mountbatten wishes to join the Club, it was decided to put his name forward for election as a member . . . under Rule 15.'

On 6 November 1947, George Malcolm Thomson was elected a member, thank goodness. So was Stephen Potter. The last of fifteen successful candidates listed on that evening was Lieutenant Philip Mountbatten RN. His letter of appreciation at his election was read at the meeting on 4 December.

Guy Boas, a member of the Garrick since 1943, had been working for some time on a short history of the Club, and this was ready in February 1948. The Committee was told that members could buy the book for 5s and that Bumpus were handling the retail sale to the general public. Two hundred copies were sold in the first month – good value, too, because it was well printed on excellent paper and well bound in red buckram at a time when austerity in book production still reigned. For this effort thanks were expressed to Colonel Oscar Viney and his firm Hazell, Watson and Viney. Appropriately, a publisher who had an unsurpassed touch with book design and production, G. Wren Howard of Jonathan Cape, was elected a member at this time; and to make up an interesting trio, so were Robert Morley and T. S. Eliot (Rule 15).

Later in 1948 a showering of members were elected, no fewer than twenty at one go, including Jack Hawkins, Alan Melville, Alec Guinness and Leslie Henson, all drama, and a solitary artist (but worth a dozen) Augustus John.

Once again reflecting the war of attrition carried on month after month, year after year, by members' wives, the question of ladies dining in the coffee room on Saturdays and Sundays at up to seven tables, and their presence in the morning room between 7 and 11 pm, came up for discussion. The revisionists won again, but lost a few months later when a member, pushing his luck, recklessly suggested ladies should dine *every* night – except sacred Thursdays, traditionally members-only evenings. The film producer Cavalcanti asked if he could use a facsimile of the Club lounge for a scene in his new movie. In spite of the film's title, *For Them that Trespass*, the Committee assented.

David Farrer, ignoring past outrage, again brought up the question of a bar – 'but it will increase revenue,' he pleaded. It took no less a figure than Sir Patrick Hastings to kill the proposal this time.

Neither the house nor the general Committee appear to have done anything in 1950 – or nothing of any historical importance. But window boxes were installed for the first time, which ever since have softened the harsh and soot-begrimed front facade.

With the death of the Club's patron, King George VI, it was decided to invite the honorary member H.R.H. the Duke of Edinburgh to take over. At the meeting on 6 November a letter saying that he would be glad to do so was read out; and exactly a year later the new secretary reported that the house committee had completed all arrangements for a dinner in the Duke of Edinburgh's honour on Sunday 8 November 1953.

This new secretary was none other than Commander E.S. Satterthwaite RN (retd) whose gaunt features, mariner's keen eye, bluff but punctilious manner, lent a very special tone to the Club for precisely twenty years. The Royal Navy trains its officers to foster good relations with the lower deck and Satters from his first day attracted the respect and affection of the Club's staff, which became a priceless asset. As for members – he knew them all by name from the day they were elected, watched over their comfort – and when necessary their comportment.

Commander Satterthwaite was stylish and accomplished at the billiards table, and ensured that this remote outpost was at least explored by members. At the same time the charge for accidentally cutting the cloth was raised to two guineas – 4 February 1954.

This, fortunately, did not raise much revenue. But, with the new secretary – or soon after – came a renewed onslaught on

[49]

reactionary beliefs about a bar. ' "This is ridiculous," I remember saying when I first came to the club,' Satters recalls today. 'All these waiters rushing around with trays and members pushing bells.'

And it was the Commander's weight behind the reforming steamroller that got it going at last, at the A.G.M. in April 1954. There was inevitably a long, noisy discussion, but in the end there was only one dissenting vote, a lawyer's. Appropriately, Kenneth More, who was to decorate this bar almost daily when in London until his untimely death, was elected a member three weeks earlier. So was Rex Harrison, but we did not see so much of him. Membership, by the way, had crept over the six hundred mark again in 1954. It was noted sardonically that the members – judges, lawyers and barristers especially – who had been most vehement against a bar, were called to it at once and were never again seen pressing a bell for a drink.

The use of Club writing paper for letters to *The Times* on any political theme has often been raised and it has invariably been the Committee's opinion that the practice is undesirable. Long, long ago, when the Club was still in King Street, the need arose for the Committee to inform a member 'that their attention having been directed to some recent letters addressed by you to the newspapers, they venture to request that in further communications to the newspapers upon your private affairs, shall be made in such a manner as that the name of the Garrick Club may not be introduced'.[15] When two members wrote a letter with a political note in it, Basil Dean, the impresario, wrote to the secretary to complain, and again a notice was posted drawing members' attention 'to the undesirability of such procedure'. Some members think it ought to be incorporated in the rules.

A new chef had been appointed at almost the same time as Commander Satterthwaite as secretary, and the pair worked together in harmony for almost fifteen years. Mr Leonard Coleman was a great lobster man, having six live lobsters delivered every morning, mostly for his widely-famed Lobster Cardinale. He was a kind man, and for a chef, very modest, referring to his 'lash-ups' rather than making a great mystique about the business of cooking. 'He had no respect for persons but if he liked you he liked you,' Judge Billy Hughes (1954) comments, and recalls bringing his son into the Club briefly on his way back to Eton. Coleman, prowling about the hall, took one glance at him and said, 'Hullo, you're looking very thin. Get your dad to bring you in here and I'll do you a lash-up.'

Perhaps Mr Coleman's peak, the accolades ringing loudly in his kitchen, occurred in July 1960 when, 'it was noted' at the July meeting 'with pleasure that the Chef, Mr Coleman, had been selected to represent Great Britain at the forthcoming culinary competition to be held at Frankfurt . . .'

As another Garrick centenary loomed, this time the centenary of the Club's premises, the membership lurched over the 800 mark. And how was the occasion to be celebrated? As usual, by many members eating and drinking a great deal at the same time and in the same place, and all talking without pause. There should, recommended the house committee, be a dinner on 6 July and a soirée on the following day. Drew Middleton, the American writer and correspondent, a member and friend of the Garrick, and of Britain, for so many years, should be asked to reply to the toast of the Club to be proposed by the chairman.

Two somewhat quirky suggestions came before Committee members in the mid-1960s. Perhaps they reflected the swinging decade we were all undergoing to the background beat of the Beatles: that there should be a record of members' professions, and members should provide *photographs* of themselves for sticking into albums to be placed in the bar (they are still there). There was a time, old members sighed, when gentlemen did not have professions, and if they did, could never be induced to discuss such an embarrassing necessity. But to have them on record, and as for cultivating the personality with pictures of yourself on public display! But to emphasise that there were some depths to which the Garrick would not yet descend, the proposed introduction of a 'fruit machine' was thrown out by both house and general Committee.

However, the Committee did agree (7 November 1968) 'that the Secretary shall use his discretion in permitting ladies to enter the Club in the evening wearing trousers. The guiding principle being that a lady who had obviously gone home and changed for the occasion should certainly be admitted.' 'Obviously' being the key word to this ruling, or did the secretary ask?

On a more suitable and traditional note, Sir Donald Wolfit, whose nineteenth century style and profile always seemed to recall Garrick's, and the Garrick Club's vintage years, wrote to the Committee asking that it should 'keep in mind the provision of Rule 1 which states that the Club is interested in the general patronage of the drama which I interpret as requiring all members to attend the theatre regularly'. It was a fine last rousing gesture; he died shortly after.

The loss of Sir Donald Wolfit was offset in the early days of the new decade – 1970 – by the election of Sir John Gielgud under Rule 15. A year later, as a result of the unhappy demise of A. A. Milne's widow, the Club was to receive 25% of the earnings of his children's books – the 'Pooh royalties' as they were at once and affectionately called. The total, the Committee was told, would probably amount to around £50,000 pa. It has often exceeded that figure, and the bear's honeypot has sweetened the Garrick's finances for fifteen years. That a room has been named after that generous writer is only a small token of the Club's appreciation.

The death of Sir Noël Coward brought a further bounty to the Club in the shape of his visitors' book which he had kept since the early 1930s. Mr Cole Lesley, one of his executors, said that the only condition of the gift was that the Club would never sell it, an assurance given with electric speed.

By 1975 ladies were to be found in the bar on Sunday evenings, and dining in the coffee room even on Thursday evenings, using the front staircase, penetrating to almost every corner of the Club. The contest, except for the final victory of equal membership, was almost over.

The Committee, who had helped bring about this momentous state of affairs, included Sir John Clements, Marius Goring,

Raymond Huntley (drama), Sir Michael Havers, Sir Melford Stevenson and Lord Justice Russell (chairman) for the law, and Robin Day on behalf of television, and The Truth. At the 6 February 1975 meeting, the chairman regretted that this would be the last meeting which the present secretary would attend. Commander Satterthwaite had retired at the end of 1972, since when Major Norman Thackeray, of the related service the Royal Marines, had presided over the running of the Club. Major Thackeray had the unusual record of escaping from the sinking battleship *Royal Oak* in Scapa Flow through a torpedo tube at the age of fourteen. It made a graphic story, but I think he told it only once when I happened to be at the bar beside him. He was succeeded by the present occupant of the secretary's office, Martin Harvey – a suitable name to follow 'Thackeray', and a blessing beyond all praise.

Over the years there have been overtures to buy the Club from various sources. In March 1975 another approach was made suggesting that the government would like to buy the premises to make it into a National Theatre Museum, 'including Garrick paintings and treasures in the display'. Somerset House would then be made into a Turner Gallery, 'and the Garrick would have enough money to set itself up in new premises'. 'Ho, ho!' a member of the Committee roared when he could find his breath. The discussion was brief, the outrage extended.

Today there are, as in 1831, three Trustees and a general Committee of twenty-four members who serve for four years, resulting in an annual election of six new members. This Committee discusses the general working of the Club, acts as a voice for members, in praise or complaint, and considers candidates as they come up for election. The last is the Committee's most important function, and in the words of John Timbs at the head of this chapter, it 'is compelled to exercise a very vigilant care'. There was a minor wave of black-balling again not long ago, but the customary tightening up of arrangements has led to this unhappy business becoming a rarity again, mainly by the use of quiet suggestion to proposers and seconders that there may be some opposition to their candidate's election.

The house committee consists of eight members, a chairman nominated by the Trustees, four of whom are already members of the general Committee. The definition of the remaining three is that 'in the opinion of the general committee they are especially qualified to assist in the management of the club'. A member who happens to be chairman of a large building company, for example, may be specially qualified to give advice on specifications and estimates for roof repairs. The house committee supervises finances, the maintenance of the Club premises, staff conditions and service, and remains in close liaison with the general Committee. It is the most demanding of the Committees. The wine committee makes different demands, is the butt of much mirth and sardonic comment, and does a thoroughly good job. Then there is the works of art committee, and card and library committees, whose functions are self-evident, unlike the property committee.

G. K. Chesterton once wrote:

> Lord Lilac thought it rather rotten
> That Shakespeare should be quite forgotten,
> And therefore got on a Committee
> With several chaps out of the City

The good Lord Lilac may be assured that one item the Garrick committees do not have on their agendas is the need to remember Shakespeare, whose bust is so prominently displayed and for whom the annual dinner has recently been revived.

3

Members

'We are a merry family,
We are! We are! We are!'★

ON 19 APRIL 1926 Sean O'Casey was whisked along to the
Garrick for lunch by his fellow Irishman friend and producer,
James Fagan. O'Casey was on his first visit to London, wide-eyed
with wonder, and 'in British kindliness of heart'¹ made an honorary member of the Club to make him feel at home while he settled
down. This privilege was the work of Fagan, that 'kindly, lovable
man, widely read and extremely cultured',² who had been a pillar
and a Committee member of the Garrick for many years.

Resting in the hall at the top of the stairs, according to O'Casey,
was 'a great wreath of brass and silver-gilt, its brightness blasted
by a big black bow'. It honoured Sir Squire Bancroft who had
died that very morning of O'Casey's first entry into the Club Bancroft had loved for years; loved and served, you could say; for over
this period he had chaired countless meetings, acted as Trustee,
helped to select secretaries and staff, on occasion had held the
institution together during crises. If Fagan was a corps commander,
Bancroft was the C-in-C, 1869–1926; O'Casey a temporary acting
lieutenant.

Born in London on 14 May 1841, Bancroft became one of the
great actor-managers, a tall, distinguished man of the theatre,
reaching his peak in the late Victorian era, being knighted in 1897.
One evening in 1883 Bancroft played the lead in *Fedora* in the
Garrick's coffee room before an actor-only audience of 100 in
honour of Sir Henry Irving's departure on his first visit to America.

★ 'In those early days at the Garrick (1865), with Arthur Sullivan, Frederick
Clay, Harry Weldon, Captain Hawley Smart the novelist, and one or two
others, we could, indeed, have adapted [this] chorus of a once popular song . . .
And so we were.' Sir Frank Burnand, *Records and Reminiscences*, 1904, ii, p. 18.

[55]

Phil May drew the supposed finale to that unique occasion, depicting a greatly-the-worse-for-wear Irving, J. L. Toole and Bancroft himself.

In 1867 Bancroft married Marie Effie Wilton, who had been on the stage since early childhood and had played with Macready on his farewell performance in the provinces, as Fleance in *Macbeth*, Prince Arthur in *King John*, Perdita in Barnabas Brough's extravaganza, *The Winter's Tale*, and in burlesque at the Strand in the plays of H. J. Byron. It was an ideal marriage between two talented and extremely nice people, and they entertained their friends constantly at A1 The Albany.

Bancroft's opinion was widely sought after at the Garrick. His only son, who married Sir John Hare's daughter, tells of lunch at the Garrick on the day after a controversial matinée of *Macbeth* with Arthur Bourchier – also a member – in the name part. Young Bancroft had already heard at breakfast that morning his mother's caricature of the dagger scene – 'My dear, it was like the "Jolly Waterman".' Now at lunch, surrounded by members who had all been at the performance, young Bancroft saw his father arrive. 'Ah, here's Sir Squire,' he was greeted. 'He'll settle the matter. What did *you*, Sir Squire, think of Bourchier's *Macbeth*?'

'There was a long pause while he adjusted his eyeglass,' recalled young George Bancroft, 'and at length he answered very solemnly, "Parts of it were good and parts of it were not so good. The whole question is whether what was good was good enough".'³

> Farewell, Macready, since this night we part,
> Go, take thine honours home . . .

In his *Reminiscences and Selections from his Diaries and Letters*, Macready has an early if negative reference to the Club that meant so much to him:

April 23rd 1833, Shakespeare's Birthday. – On this day I was to have met the Garrick Club at dinner in honour of Shakespeare's birthday, and intended to have felt their dispositions towards erecting some memorial to Mrs Siddons; instead of which . . .

and he informs his readers of the poor state of his health. He was not much better a year later, and was straining his weak reserves playing *Coriolanus*. Like countless actors for the past 150 years, on his arrival at the Garrick he settled down at once to read his notices regardless of the rest of the world, and the Club.

> I went to the Garrick to read the newspapers, which were all very favourable to me, and to dine – saw Collier, Taylor, Bartley and several others. I fear I carried the effort at modesty, which the pride of success puts on, upon my deportment, but it was against my will if it was so.

The admirable Macready continued to press the Garrick for a memorial to his heroine, Mrs Siddons, and took advantage of a speech he made at a Literary Fund dinner at the Club on the hot evening of 3 July 1834:

> To the very last moment I persisted in thinking over and repeating my speech and went at last to the dinner at the Garrick Club. Saw Fladgate in the drawing room, who agreed to bring forward the business of Mrs Siddons' monument, and I engaged that Talfourd should press it forward. Introduced to Messrs Thackeray, Graves, Bredel, Maynard, Maitland, Brown, Murphy, Palmer ... There was venison & co and excellent wines. Talfourd proposed my health in a speech as eloquent as it was kind, which says all for it that truth and admiration can wish to say. I answered it as well as I could with self-possession, but under strong nervous excitement. We had some very good songs from James Smith and Blood, and the evening was very pleasant ... Shortly after Thackeray and one or two others dropped away ...

But enough members remained to carry a resolution that '£50 be voted instantly' for the Mrs Siddons fund; then, well satisfied with the evening, Macready departed for his chambers, leaving the hard core of revellers at 1 am to their broiled bones and iced champagne.

The Talfourd to whom Macready frequently refers in his diaries,

[57]

was Mr Justice Talfourd, chairman of the Garrick Committee and a close friend of Macready after he acted favourably as an arbiter in his row with Covent Garden.

From the *Pall Mall Gazette* we read of a rather later famous figure of the theatre, the manager John Hollingshead, who made the Gaiety famous:

> The portrait gallery of the Garrick Club would certainly be incomplete if it did not include Mr John Hollingshead. Few men have figured more prominently than he in the history of the English stage for the past thirty years. It may be doubted, however, whether his activity has been on the whole so beneficent as Mr Clement Scott would make out. He has 'multiplied theatres' – but, in the matter of theatres, 'multiplication (beyond a certain point) is vexation'. He has 'raised dramatic pay' – was it not rather the Bancrofts who did that? He has 'invented matinées' – a doubtful boon; he has 'abolished fees' – for that we certainly owe him gratitude; and (this Mr Scott forgets to mention) he imported the Comédie Française. So far so good; but when we come to the *per contra*, what do we find? He has invented 'three act burlesque dramas', and has catered cynically to the 'masher', the loafer, and the rake. It is instructive to reflect that, with all his practicality, 'Practical John' has not been greatly or permanently successful. It is the managers with a certain artistic ideal – the Bancrofts and Irvings of the time – who have done true service and reaped great reward.

James Planché's name appears as an early Committee member, a 37-year-old writer who was soon to publish his *History of British Costumes*. Everybody loved Planché but one suspects he was the Garrick's pioneer bore – and veteran bore because he was a member for fifty years. 'I was once with him at a country house where he was most agreeable,' a fellow member recalls. 'But there was a nobleman of very plain and blunt manners, who would complain loudly of "old Planché's prosy yarns". He would unceremoniously interrupt him, but scarcely listened. On one occasion, the *raconteur* was relating one of his "leetle anecdotes" . . . when the host said something to a lady half-way down the table; this brought a reply, others joined in, and poor Planché was left planté . . . I see his mortified air as he said, "My lord, you are not attending to me".'[6]

Planché designed and supervized the costumes for Charles Kemble's *King John* eight years before the Garrick was founded, with Kemble as a founder member, too. Planché was clearly a man of many talents if that of a raconteur was not one of them. 'Much of Gilbert's libretti for the Savoy operas was based on or suggested by the texts of Planché's extravaganzas,'[7] writes one authority. And he wrote the libretto for Weber's *Oberon* amongst many others, including the book for an opera on the siege of Calais for Mendelssohn, though 'the composer, changing his mind, grew cool and declined to use it'.[8]

Thackeray was an early but not a founder member. Planché found him 'a slim young man, rather taciturn and not displaying any particular love or talent for literature. Drawing appears to be his favourite amusement,' he observed, 'and he often sat by my side while I was reading or writing, covering any scrap of paper with the most spirited sketches and amusing caricatures'. 'At twenty you know,' he once reminded his mother, 'we all thought I was a genius at drawing'.[9] Thackeray's pen, according to Planché, led to one member he thought objectionable resigning – and not by words from his pen either. Thackeray drew numerous unflattering and back view caricatures of the poor fellow, leaving them about the club for all to see and immediately recognise. 'The member bore his persecution for a long time with good humour, but at last one rather too "strong" a counterfeit presentment made him withdraw.'[10]

Although one of the cornerstones of the Garrick for so many years, Thackeray was never popular with the general run of members. However, one of them, W. Pryce Maunsell, wrote in his defence many years later:

I think he was in some degree dissatisfied with literature as a profession. He used to pay court to the celebrated barrister, Mr Willes, afterwards the judge, Sir James Shaw Willes, who, though a most brilliant, clever man seemed to most as inferior to the great writer of the age. I remember once, in the smoking room, during the Crimean War, Willes said that he hated all these accounts of our failures, as written by Mr Russell in *The Times*. 'I', said Thackeray, 'would conceal nothing about myself or others. My door is always open.' Like Byron, he had a habit of making himself out worse than he really was – this, I think, from a hatred of hypocrites and hypocrisy. He hated rich fools, having tasted poverty before he wrote *Vanity Fair*. One man told me that he once said that he had a wife and two children, and another coming, and that he often did not know where to look for a five-pound note. Another told me that when he had men in his chamber, and Thackeray was there, he was so satirical that the men refused to go if he was to be there. But all who knew him well agreed that under this cynical aspect he was really kind, generous, and amiable, and in some degree in this he resembled Dr Johnson.[11]

The title 'father of the Garrick' has traditionally been reserved for Francis 'Papa' Fladgate. Of all the founder members who guided the Club through its first difficult years, Fladgate's influence and energy were not matched even by Francis Mills, Colonel de Bathe and the Committee chairman for so many years, Lord Tenterden. Courteous, gentle, kindly, especially to new and young members, he was the most loved member and one of the longest-serving in the Garrick's history.

Frank Fladgate inherited a modest fortune from his father, 'an attorney in Essex', but this was whittled away over the years by acts of kindness and generosity and he was not well off when he died in his nineties. He was seven when he watched Nelson's funeral procession passing slowly down the Strand. The club was sixty years old, and he a member of it for that time, when he died. Although he became a barrister as a young man, he never practised, the Garrick and the theatre being his whole life.

Percy Fitzgerald wrote of 'Papa' Fladgate in 1904, a decade after his death.

> It was a constant delight for me to get into talk with this veteran, who had mixed in the theatrical world in all its stages, and had known Kemble and Siddons and members of the Garrick School. His recollections were of the most interesting kind, for he had been a shrewd observer. Sometimes I would meet him in the library poring over a play which he could not read, and most grateful was he on my volunteering to do this office for him ... I thought it rather fortunate to be with a man who would show you in very vivid fashion how John Kemble played 'The Stranger', giving all his business, tones of voice, &c.[12]

Older members today will remember that paragon of kindness and courtliness, Sir Julian Hall, Bart. In his deep interest in the theatre, his concern for new young members, his prodigious knowledge of drama, he had much in common with Frank Fladgate, and no doubt they are chattering away backstage about Kemble, Irving, Olivier and Richardson, and the best *Lear* they ever saw.

Frank Fladgate lived at Brompton, and as he advanced into his late 70s he found the journey to Garrick Street more and more testing; but like others in their dotage we have known, the Garrick became a survival symbol, a life-saving antidote to loneliness. But, oh those front steps! Mr Marrable did not take account of the effect of old age on octogenarian legs. But old Frank made the top step at last, with some help from the porters, and then ... 'His quaint old-fashioned figure ... his antique high satin stock, the shade over his eye, his stoop even – how familiar and matter-of-course was all this! Always good-humoured, full of an amiable *bonhomie* to all his "children" whom he could scarcely see, hobbling about and clinging with desperation almost to his beloved old haunt...'[13]

The Rev Richard Barham described Frank Fladgate as 'one of the most polished gentlemen and good-natured persons I ever met'.[14] The same cannot be said of Barham himself, even if he was a more vivid figure. Ten years older than Frank Fladgate, he died at the relatively early age of 57 and saw only the first thirteen years of the Garrick as a founder member. Barham was a sort of comic canon, educated at St Paul's and Brasenose, more occupied with snappy and not always charitable conversation and 'the grotesque or frankly comic treatment of medieval legend'[15] than his duties as priest of the Chapel Royal and a minor canon at St Paul's Cathedral.

Fitzgerald described Barham as 'the sayer of good things and the haunter of the Garrick'. Richard Garnett called him 'The associate of men of wit and gaiety, making no pretension to any extraordinary strictness of conduct, he passed through life with perfect credit as a clergyman, and universal respect as a member of society.' But then Garnett wrote this without the benefit of reading the MS of Barham's *The Garrick Club*. This was written in the 1840s and described in frank and unrestrained terms his contemporary fellow members, not all of them as flatteringly as Fladgate. John Forster is 'a low scribbler without an atom of talent and totally unused to the society of gentlemen'. Sir Wyndham Anstruther, Bart is 'a regular scamp', Samuel Arnold 'quite a sot', the Hon. R. Carlton 'a clergyman and apparently half crazy', while Charles Ellis is 'a half mad attorney who was constantly drunk and as constantly quarrelsome'.

Besides these sweet little vignettes of his fellow members, there are scraps of history in this book, like: 'Resigned his situation at the Club because they gave a dinner to their President, Lord Mulgrave, which he absurdly enough chose to consider a political demonstration, whereas if there be any politics at all in it, they tend much more to ultra Toryism than Whiggery.' Then we learn the sad story of the 'inimitable comic actor' Charles Mathews, who was also famous for his *At Home* – 'a form peculiar to himself which has been described as "a whole play in the person of one man".'[16] It seems that 'the Club purchased for £1,000 a collection of theatrical pictures which had cost him more than four times that amount. Bentley (the publisher and fellow member) gave £500 to his widow for materials for his life, and £500 to Hook to edit them, but the latter afterwards gave up his part of the bargain, and Bentley gave Mrs M. another £100 to do it herself in 1838.'

Barham is a curious character, uneven and unpredictable. He could not have been wholly easy company, and the notes on his fellow members reflect his changing moods and extravagant opinions.

There were plenty of comedian members in those early days, which made the Garrick as noisy and probably even more entertaining than it is today. One was Tyrone Power (no, not the movie actor), son of an Irish strolling player. 'A handsome, high-spirited man with thick curling hair, a rich brogue and a fine singing voice'[17] who played in farces and comedies, some written by himself. Much loved in America, too, he was drowned returning from a tour there when the SS *President* went down in a storm in 1841.

At the heavy end of drama, Charles Kemble was the most famous founder member. He also served for many years on the Committee where his deafness was an inconvenience and embarrassment. He was once observed reading while a tremendous thunderstorm descended on central London. At its height he was seen to look up and remark, 'I think we are going to have *thunder*.' There is an early portrait of Kemble as Macbeth in the club 'giving us an idea of the old declamatory, "striding" or strident style of declaiming an heroic character'.[18] It was painted by a clever young artist called Kearsley before he went mad and spent the rest of his life in an asylum.

Thomas 'Tommy' Duncombe was probably the most popular man of the theatre (and M.P.) among the 'very early' members. He was certainly popular after roughing up a newspaper proprietor who thrived on scurrilous attacks on theatre people, a Mr Westmacott of the Sunday *Age*. Westmacott approached Duncombe at the Drury Lane Theatre, and asked him how he was doing. 'I am surprised, sir,' Duncombe retorted hotly, 'that you should think of addressing me when you are abusing me constantly in your paper, and I desire that when you do speak to me you will take off your hat'. So saying, he took it off for him and threw it on the ground.

The newspaperman then drew off his gloves, but Duncombe

got in first with two short stabs to the head. The parties were separated, and there was talk of a duel. But when Tommy Duncombe appeared at the Garrick the next day, Planché and Mathews were among those awaiting him on the steps who gave him a cheer for giving the fellow a good knocking about.

Two firm upholders of civil behaviour and adherance to the rules of those early days – and *they* would never have lowered themselves to fisticuffs in a public place – were Colonel Sir Henry de Bathe and Sir Charles Taylor. They were not very popular in their time, which was very long. We should not have put up with them today, and not only because they 'combined an airy cynicism with a contemptuous condescension of manner'. Stiff, Committee member autocrats, the only evidence of informality they evidenced was in calling Thackeray 'Thack'. But these three did form a triumverate of severity which prevented jolly drunken riots late in the evening among the vast majority of happy, compatible and ebullient members who made life fun and were the true essence of the King Street Garrick.

> Our hearty laughter, as we pretty regularly dined together [Sir Frank Burnand recalled] brought down upon us the thunder of Sir Charles Taylor, the Jupiter Tonans of the club, in the shape of a severe message, delivered to us by Farman, the steward, a hard, stolid man, considered rather as 'a creature' of Sir Charles's, then the head servant of the club. Most of our fellow-members and seniors were inclined to sympathise with us, Sir Charles being looked upon as rather an autocrat, and therefore not generally popular. However, as 'Goody' in the opera of Midas was requested 'to moderate the rancour of her tongue', so we, being peremptorily required to tone down our merriment, complied: we 'ate the leek, and eke' we used strong, but not loud, language concerning our tyrannical oppressor.[19]

Charles Dickens was not one of the clubbable members, not one of the midnight smoking room crowd; and the Garrick was far more enthusiastic about having 'Boz' as a member than Dickens himself at being one. In 1836 Bentley, the publisher of *Miscellany* which Dickens was editing, at last prevailed upon him to allow his name to go forward as a candidate.

> I have been worried and worried again and again by Bentley [Dickens wrote to his friend, the comedian J. P. Hartley] . . . to allow myself to be proposed as a member of the Garrick. I have consented to undergo the honor and am to be proposed forthwith – by whom I don't know out of the number. However, when the proposition *does* take place, I should like you to second it. I think you will have no objection, and I should very much like your doing it.

On 21 January 1837, then, Dickens's name came before the Committee as 'Charles Dickens Esq, of Furnival's Inn'. The proposer was Dr J. Gideon Millengen 'of Bordeaux', the author of *The Beehive* and *The State of Learning*. It is extremely unlikely that any member of that Committee – Mr Hook in the chair, Fladgate, Durrant, Robins, Beloe, Douglas and Charles Kemble – had failed to read the tenth monthly part of *Pickwick Papers* by 'Boz' which had just been published; all about Christmas at Dingley Dell and the story of Gabriel Grub. The Committee, according to custom, examined the candidate's page, saw the name of John Forster and of Sergeant Talfourd, who was to become the original of Traddles in *David Copperfield*, and elected him. As a sort of double courtesy, the next item on the agenda was to resolve that 'the club should subscribe to [Dickens's] *Miscellany*'.

But the Club itself was only mentioned once in Dickens's future writing, and that was in a new edition of *Sketches by Boz* anonymously under the title 'The Theatrical Young Gentlemen', who imagine that 'to be a member of the Garrick Club, and see so many actors in their plain clothes, must be one of the highest gratifications that the world can bestow'.

Dickens's membership of nineteen years in all was not continuous. He was one of those oddities, a member who can't make up his mind. He resigned for the first time after twenty-two months in co-dudgeon with Macready. Talfourd persuaded him to rejoin in January 1844. This time he lasted longer, resigning in December

[65]

1849, for no known reason, after supporting the candidature of two of his close friends, John Leech and Augustus Egg. The Club sorely missed him, and his ever-growing status, and persuaded him to rejoin on 1 April 1854, backed by over fifty members, and soon made him a Committee member. He presided over the Shakespeare dinner and apparently made 'by far the best after-dinner speaker I ever heard', according to his friend Edmund Yates. He enjoyed this third term more than the others.

As Charles Dickens towered above all other early Garrick writers, to the chagrin of Thackeray but not to Wilkie Collins (second and third respectively), so Henry Irving was the giant of the theatre from the mid-victorian years. An earlier Garrick historian writes of his *domination* by his mere presence.

Domination, electric, almost mesmeric, was the profession, the life-force, of that stupendous and uncanny personality. It was little wonder that the man who had frozen the blood of audiences as Richard III, had petrified all beholders as Mathias and Mephistopheles, and had wrung the nation's heart as Charles I, Dr Primrose, and Thomas à Becket, and at the same time had contrived to remain 'always Irving', should have permeated, even after he had left the dressing-room, any human company which contained him. But did it contain him?

He was there in bodily presence, at times contributing an incisive remark, sometimes content to puff cigar after cigar in silence.

But mostly he talked; and it was Irving at the head of the long table whom members recalled after he had gone, talking, talking, talking, to a large but to him anonymous audience, identified only when some exhausted neighbour plucked up courage to retire. 'I regret, sir,' he would then say, 'that you are fatigued by our company'.

Sir Rupert Hart-Davis, a member himself for forty years, recalls William Nicholson, the painter, telling him of a packed after-theatre supper in the 1890s when Irving held sway at the head of the table as usual and about fifty other conversations were going on. 'In the midst of all the chatter there was one of those sudden silences ("angels' visits" they used to be called), in which Irving was suddenly heard declaiming loudly and with emphasis on each word, "*Nansen* – stands – the – *cold* – well". Then the chatter started again.'[21]

Once, it is on record, Irving was actually out-talked, but this was only out of courtesy as host. The explorer H. M. Stanley, of Stanley and Livingstone, was in London and much fêting included an evening at the Garrick as a guest. At the coffee-and-cigar stage Irving at last yielded the conversation to him: 'My dear fellow, you must tell us about your adventures – your wanderings – in – um – Africa. Now – gentlemen – will you listen – to – er – Mr Stanley. His experiences are most interesting, *most* interesting.'

Sir Francis Burnand, the only member besides Irving to last out the laboured and protracted account that followed, watched Irving slowly succumb to the soporific sound of his monotonous voice. 'Partially disappearing under the table, he was stretched out at full length, his head supported by the top rail of the chair-back, in which position he appeared to be listening as carefully as a judge, with his eyes shut, to a lengthy speech of counsel. Occasionally he would nod; and lest a false construction should be placed on this Homeric action, he would open his eyes, murmur approval, give a glance, somewhat sardonically, round the table, and then relapse into his attitude of attention . . .'[22]

Irving's dominance of the Garrick towards the end of the Victorian era and the early years of the twentieth century was emphasised by the club's general loss of sparkle during his greatest years, enlivened briefly in 1882 by the Honorary Membership of seventeen Comédie Française actors, including Sacha Guitry's father, Lucien Germain.

Roughly, from 1880 until shortly before the First World War, was the Garrick's dark age, when the very old members could, for once with justice, mutter sadly amongst themselves about things not being what they used to be. As one member wrote in 1904, the club's nadir, 'The Garrick, in its early days, had been well stored with wits and humorists of the first class, leavened also by the more "Bohemian" members of the theatrical profession, pleasant soldiers and jovial peers. But in these later times it has become more like the usual type found in Clubland . . .'[23] Even the list of members has a dour look to it.

Bert Thomas in Clubland

NO. 1. THE GARRICK

The Savage Thespian, mould of Hamlet's form, Here finds a barn the groundlings cannot storm.

4

Encore

YOU MIGHT NOT think it, judged by the noise level at the Garrick sometimes, but there are and always have been in every generation, 'club listeners', who observe, admire and occasionally chip in to keep the talk rolling; and very essential they are, too. One of these, a frequent attender around the turn of the century, was W.L. Courtney, a Fellow of New College, Oxford, and a bit of a ponderous bore, too, I would surmise. But he left in his memoirs sketches of his Garrick contemporaries of the Edwardian era, some of which are worth preserving. For example:

There was Henry Kemble – a good man and true, though a little rough perhaps in manner and not always polite to those with whom he disagreed. He had a great and wonderful acquaintance with poetry of all kinds, and he held a high position of authority in any debate on things theatrical. He was an exceedingly shrewd man, with an intuitive knowledge of character which was quite remarkable . . .

Or there was W.S. Gilbert, who used to display an extremely poignant skill in discovering the weak points in a person's armour. But he steadily got mellower and more kind as his years advanced, until eventually to be talking with W.S. Gilbert did not mean that you went away eternally humiliated and disgraced . . .

Or there was another man, who also knew how to hit hard – Joe Comyns Carr – an exceedingly clever talker, with a natural and spontaneous brightness of his own which rendered memorable every word-combat in which he engaged. No one especially cared to argue with Joe Carr, because as a subtle adversary and sometimes as *advocatus diaboli* he won a facile triumph by the quickness of his repartee . . .

Harry Irving was a dear friend of mine, and all that he did was to me a fresh source of joy. He was a very true friend, and, so far as I am concerned, his friendship began when we left Marlborough and came to New College, Oxford. His father, Sir Henry Irving, had sent him mainly to be my pupil, and I soon found that my responsibility was all the lighter because Harry had so clearly defined and established a personality. He was much older than some of the young men around him – older not in years, but in mental experience; and he had the wit to accommodate himself to the circumstances which he found around him, so far as they did not interfere with his intense devotion to art. . . . The splendid thing about Harry Irving – or perhaps I should say one of the splendid things – was his immense and unshakable belief in the dignity, the grace and power of the true artist . . .

George Alexander did not, I think, come so often to the Garrick Club as his fellow-actors. For one reason he had a certain delicacy of physique which prevented him from enjoying late hours. His also was not altogether an expansive nature. Indeed, he was reserved and shy, and, like most men who are shy, he had at times a manner somewhat cold and repellent . . .

Two actors who belong to the Victorian era – Sir Squire Bancroft and Sir Charles Wyndham – I must refer to. Bancroft is happily alive, and is wearing the crown of his years with remarkable ease. His lifetime covers no small portion of recent dramatic history, and everyone speaks affectionately of 'Old B.' because of his kindliness, his essential humanity and his remarkable personality. Charles Wyndham died a few years ago, and by his death we lost a brilliant comedian, a man who was more essentially an actor of comedy than any of those figures which the Victorian era produced. . . . He did not come so often to the Garrick as other actors, mainly because he found that, nervous as he was by nature, he would be adding to the trial of his nerves if he partook of supper. He was troubled with sleeplessness at a certain period in his career, and in order to conquer this he used frequently to walk home to St John's Wood instead of sharing in the animated conversations of the Club. Light drawing-room comedy at its best was his forte, and though many young actors have done their best to imitate him, his place in theatrical history is still unfilled.

John Hare was a well-known and popular figure in the Club. He used to spend many afternoons in the card-room, was much interested in Club affairs, and was always ready to take a hand in anything that would be likely to promote its interests. He was essentially a comedian, a comedian of a very fine type, who discovered that his most successfule role was the impersonation of old men . . .

Johnston Forbes-Robertson belongs also to the Victorian era. Happily he is still with us, though he acts but rarely. He was a well graced actor, a man of great distinction and charm, whose performances in romantic parts carried away his audiences, illustrated and expounded as they were by one of the most beautiful speaking voices that we have had on the stage. He acted, as everybody will remember, a good deal with Irving at the Lyceum. One of the triumphs of his career was *The Passing of the Third Floor Back*. He is essentially a Shakespearian actor, who knew how to manage blank verse throughout a period in which actors and actresses have been somewhat negligent in this matter.

By 1914, who do we find? First, for literature, J. M. Barrie and Kenneth Grahame, Max Pemberton and Hugh Walpole – and also, incidentally, that lively-minded American publisher Charles Scribner. Representing the theatre, we see the names of Gerald du Maurier, Nigel Playfair, Sir Herbert Beerbohm Tree, A. E. 'Mattie' Matthews and Howard Wyndham.

A. E. Matthews was often described as 'lovable and mischievous'. He was certainly a very kind man, conscious of the feelings of others. John Gielgud recalls him many years later. 'I directed him once in a play and we got on together very well at the rehearsals. Meeting him in the street some time afterwards I asked him where he was going. "To the Garrick Club," he replied, and then, quick as a flash, seeing by the look in my eye that I was not yet a member of that august fellowship, added, "I like the làvatories there so much. They have handles at the sides that help you to pull yourself up!"'

Bernard Partridge and Rowland Berkeley had enlivened the art side by 1914. The two Edwards – Sir Edward Carson and Edward Marshall Hall – sustained the more lively side of the legal tradition. I don't imagine they were clubbable in the Garrick meaning of the word, but as always it was a comfort to have MONEY well represented in the form of Sir Ernest Cassel, the Earl of Lonsdale, Viscount Iveagh and the Duke of Newcastle. While money-to-come-for-the-club (though it did not yet know it) was established and growing every year from Arthur Pinero.

There were also some remarkably long-lived survivors representing an earlier golden era. Squire Bancroft was still going strong when Charlie Chaplin turned up one evening, a year or two before Sean O'Casey paid his first and unhappy visit to the Garrick in 1926. The comic actor appears not to have enjoyed himself at all, or much amused the company for that matter. 'The Garrick Club had a chiaroscuro atmosphere of dark oak and oil paintings,' he wrote in his *My Autobiography*, '– a sombre haven, in which I met Sir James Barrie, E.V.Lucas, Walter Hackett, George Frampton, Edwin Lutyens, Squire Bancroft and other illustrious gentlemen.

'But I felt the evening did not quite come off . . . During dinner, Frampton, the sculptor, attempted levity and was charming; but he had difficulty in scintillating in the gloom of the Garrick Club.'³

Sir Frank Burnand, a member for almost fifty years, Edward Gould who had been elected in 1874 and Adam Kennard who had known the last *six years* of the old club house, were still going strong in 1913. The Trustees that year when the place was definitely getting jollier, were Lord Rathmore, Sir C.Rivers and Lord Burnham – Patron, the King, of course, and as secretary, the popular Charles Fitch.

Lord Burnham was still a Trustee ten years later, after the club had endured four years and four months of war, and lost a number of younger members and some of the staff. Lord Buckmaster had taken over as Senior Trustee, and dear old Squire Bancroft had attained the heights, too. Meanwhile, during that decade, the club had gained most from 'literature', and who better to head that list than A. A. Milne, later to pay back any pleasure the club gave him a million times over with his bequest; followed closely by P. G. Wodehouse, though, alas, too often away in America. Then Rafael Sabatini and, representing another aspect of the art, Charles Morgan, proposed by A. B. Walkley, seconded by Harold Child, and supported by Nigel Playfair and W. F. Clark. Daniel Macmillan upheld the tradition of having one or two publishers in the Garrick, but not too many because they were inclined to talk shop. But then so were actors, like Leon Quartermaine, Godfrey Tearle and Roland Pertwee, as were theatre managers, like Harley Granville-Barker.

Financial wizardry? You could hardly do better than Lord Howard de Walden and J. Pierpont Morgan, who somehow got in without a single signature besides those of his proposer and seconder.* Money still counted, even in the Garrick. And finally, in these halcyon immediate post-war days we find a small naval contingent, a half-flotilla of admirals, Rear-Admiral Sir W. Reginald 'Blinker' Hall, whose amazing work for naval intelligence had done so much to keep the R.N. afloat and winning, and a fellow officer in intelligence and Master Mariner of Trinity House, Rear-Admiral Sir Guy Gaunt.

There has always been a covey of Harley Street physicians and surgeons – and even some dentists – around the Garrick, a colourful lot on the whole, even eccentric. Sir Harold Gillies, to name one. He made his reputation in the First World War repairing faces. His one published work was *Plastic Surgery of the Face* (1920), and he had the wincing telegraphic address 'Plastisurg'. Among the numerous faces on which he worked was fellow Garrick member and fellow oarsman, Hamish Hamilton, whose nose took a beating

---

* This was not unusual back in the 1850s but very unusual at this time.

[73]

at prep school. Gillies was also a considerable painter and pianist and an exceptional fisherman, golfer and tennis player. A merry fellow, too, a prankster. His star performance was to drape the Garrick pictures with lavatory paper just before the arrival of the Duke of Edinburgh. Inevitably, there was a stuffy element in the hierarchy which saw to it that he did not get the customary 40-years-a-member dinner, and this hurt him very much in his old age.

So – a mixed lot, if you like, in 1923, but the Garrick was entering one of its golden eras. Members were less quarrelsome, broader-minded, in spite of Gillies's unhappy experience, enjoyed more fun and seemed prepared to let in a wider range of candidates.

One or two elderly members today recall the Garrick of the late 'twenties and early 'thirties, among them Hamish Hamilton and Melford Stevenson. Melford Stevenson, called to the Bar in 1925, was elected a member some five years later, in early 1931.

'Geoffrey Raphael and Teddy Jessel put me up,' this retired High Court Judge recalls today. 'Geoffrey later became a Metropolitan Magistrate and married Patrick Hastings's daughter. I really think this was a golden age of the Garrick. People were tremendously kind to young members. A. A. Milne, for example, was especially kind to me, and H. G. Wells, too. Allan Aynesworth looked after new actor members with great concern.

'I can recall the centenary dinner in 1931 – a great event in the Club's history. Seymour Hicks presided. Seymour was a perfect Garrick member, and very powerful personality. Old Seymour used to dominate the lounge under the stairs. When he was there gusts of laughter came out of it. He was a very, very nice man, too, never malicious, and altogether a most engaging character.'

Seymour Hicks was also responsible for suggesting membership to James Agate, a controversial figure in the theatre world, who had been only a guest when O'Casey met and took such a strong disliking to him. In his *Ego 3* Agate records for 6 February 1937: 'Seymour Hicks rang up to ask if I will join the Garrick Club. O vision entrancing! How all the other passions fleet to air!' But not for long did they. Within a week or two Agate was hearing reports of possible blackballing. William Darlington, drama critic of the

Daily Telegraph for forty-eight years in all, had put him up and had broken the sad news. So Agate wrote to Hicks on 23 February:

> I gather from your letter and Darlington's that there is a considerable amount of opposition to my election. If at any time the Committee, being unanimous, should invite me to join the Club I shall be proud and happy to become a member.
>
> But I have no intention of being snubbed by some worm-eaten old gentlemen who would probably have blackballed Garrick himself. Nor do I intend to give some extremely bad actor a toothsome bit of revenge. After all, I haven't asked to join the Club! So let us drop the whole thing ...

That was one in the eye for popular and long-honoured Seymour. And for Agate the knife was turned in the wound a few days later over lunch with Sam Eckman of Metro-Goldwyn-Mayer. Eckman was 'a delightful fellow whose idiosyncracy is to drink a liqueur brandy and smoke a cigar immediately before lunch and without having had any breakfast. As we sit down, Sam says, "Is that a Garrick Club tie you're wearing, James? I'm dining there tonight. Are you?"' Agate replied 'that it isn't and he isn't'.

Writers, publishers and book reviewers have for some reason all been considered compatible as members; even, more recently, literary agents. But drama critics have not always been considered safe company for actors and theatre managers, as if passions run deeper on the stage than on the printed page. Agate was not the only critic to have his troubles. But Sir Harold Hobson was luckier, and perhaps deserved to be. He once wrote a dreadful review of the performance and production of a play by Sir Donald Wolfit. Wolfit replied with a letter 'which began with the tremendous Johnsonian words, "If it gives you any pleasure to know that you have incurred the hatred and contempt of twenty-five hard-working and talented people, then indeed you should be a happy man." Now these hostilities do not, in most cases, last very long; they are provoked by particular occasions, and with the occasions they pass away. Two days after he had sent me this letter I met Donald in the Garrick Club, where I happened to be a guest. Did he frown and studiously avoid me? Did he attack and abuse me? On the contrary, he warmly flung his arms round me, and said, "Let me put you up for membership. The Garrick needs men like you." '

And that is how the engaging and sweet-natured Harold became a member.

Satters recalls Allan Aynesworth as an old man, coming to the Club and learning that his portrait had been completed and hung in the back room. It was not there. 'Where is my portrait?' he was heard to cry out. 'In the bar, Allan, in the bar.' So he shot up the stairs, and there it was, indeed. He glanced at it once and exclaimed, 'How insufferably vulgar!'

'The literary crowd were particularly strong then,' Melford recalled. 'Dan Macmillan started "The Burgundians", a club within the Club, nearly all literary people. They used to eat in the small dining room.' Arthur Ransome was much in evidence, too, a ferocious bridge player who also played billiards, often from 5 pm until midnight. 'The funny thing about Arthur Ransome,' says Satters today, 'is that he *loathed* anyone who whistled, and made it clear, to staff or fellow members, if he heard a whistle. But he was also a very great family friend. He was devoted to my children and at one time or another gave them signed copies of all his books.'

Reminded of the unfortunate Club secretary's defalcations at the end of 1930, Melford Stevenson recalled a hush of recent scandal in the air when he first joined. Wharton's successor 'immediately showed himself anxious to get the staff organized. He sat at a table behind the door at lunch, I recall, watching the staff with an eagle eye – very strict he was, and very just.

'In my time the distinguishing feature of the Garrick was that you were very unlucky if you went there without landing up with a very good party.' Melford, alas, can no longer make the journey; but I was able to reassure him it was just the same today.

Among those who have contributed so richly to this state of affairs is George Malcolm Thomson, once P.A. to Lord Beaverbrook.

'I'm not really a clubby person,' [he says today]. 'I had been a member of another club for a while and had not much enjoyed the experience. But I liked the Garrick enormously from the word "go" and have done for nearly forty years. I even survived an early encounter with the then Club bore, a solicitor called – shall we say – Eastern, who had been pointed out to me almost on my first visit with Percy Cudlipp.

The only empty chair at the long table was next to Eastern so I steeled myself for the encounter. As soon as I sat down he turned his chair towards me and said, 'Thomson, would you or would you not say Lord Beaverbrook is a good man?' What *was* I to say, except, 'It depends what you mean by good.'

Baddeley was the secretary at that time. He used to sit under the stairs watching members and their guests coming and going. I don't think he did very much else, and certainly the Club's finances went from bad to worse in his time.

The people I remember best were Stanley Morison – quite a chap – and the actors Donald Wolfit, Godfrey Tearle and Alastair Sim. I used to see a lot of Casey, the editor of *The Times*, too, a very, very amusing man. I think it was at my very first Club dinner that Somerset Maugham was the speaker. It was the most extraordinary speech I've ever heard in all my life. For this reason. After a while he ran out of words, just ran out. He stood quite still without changing his expression for fully three minutes while we all sat aghast and silent. Then he picked it up again and continued just as if nothing had happened.

Then I remember those early Derbys when the drink flowed like a river and in the bus coming home the songs echoed out. Food? Oh, just ordinary club food as far as I remember. This was before Coleman's time and I remember a tall, gawky chef, ex-Royal Marines, and he was quite good when he was sober.

But of course among the staff of the late 1940s I remember best Freddy Barker. Barker was more famous for his kindness and *bon mots* than his heterosexuality, and George Malcolm Thomson remembers a beautiful summer sunset, observed through the window with Barker, gazing westwards, and remarking, 'A lovely evening, sir, *and* the American Fleet's in . . .'

Drew Middleton was one of the prize catches of the mid-1950s. He is the doyen of American journalists who is liable to saunter smiling into the bar hot from Lebanon or Nicaragua and loaded with the latest crisis information – an exclusive interview with Yassar Arafat last night? – as he once used to turn up in London from the Dover cliffs after a stiff raid in 1940. Nobody can say he has aged more than ten years since then. Today he is a much-heeded, much-loved life member.

Roland Gant was 'taken in' (as they used to term it, but well before his time) a decade later than George Malcolm Thomson but still in that period when the Club was smaller and enjoyed perhaps more colour and eccentricity but, paradoxically, was more strict and formal than today. Roland Gant, like a good novelist, remembers the faces and mannerisms better than most – 'Colonel Viney, a thin face, glasses, wearing an amused alert expression, limping along on his stick – he had one of the most appallingly bent legs I've ever seen. A very pleasant, kind old man. Geoffrey Odhams was another nice old man who was also very kind.

'Then there were the regulars at the lunch-time bar – Ian Parsons, Alfred Francis, Michael Canfield, Iain Hamilton, Roger Morgan, Jep West, Romilly Whitehead, Tom Pocock. Ashley Havenden, wearing a suit with more hacking slits than you could imagine, sort of draped himself across the bar – he was very tall – a director of Crawfords, with Pip Youngman-Carter, Marjorie Allingham's husband, beside him.

'Donald Wolfit was always there when he was in London. One day, just back from Manchester, he described the view of massed television aerials he had seen from the train, uttering lugubriously, "Actors' crosses – actors' crosses". And Kenny More, of course, the jovial Jack Hawkins, Anthony Kimmins, a very big fellow, and Frank Laughton and Nigel Patrick.

'A very nice crowd in the '60s. Dear old Peter Watt. I remember him at the bar with an enormous drink ready for me. I looked at him curiously as he raised his own glass: "Jack Teagarden has just died". More drinks followed this dreadful news. And now Peter has gone, a long long time ago.'

There were a few silly hiccups and prejudices around, even then, though not so many as in the 1920s and 1930s. For instance, the present esteemed member, John Casson (1974) (shot down dive-bombing the *Scharnhorst*) recalls Sir Seymour Hicks blackballing his father, Lewis, in 1924 during the run of the first *Saint Joan*: 'We are not going to have any bloody socialists in the Garrick,' he declared. But towards the end of another German war when Lewis Casson was head of the Drama Department at C.E.M.A., the Committee, at the instigation of old Hicks, asked if he would like to join. Meeting him by chance, Lewis Casson feigned indecision. 'Yes, I'll think about it, Seymour.' He did join, and in his late 80s used to come in for lunch on Tuesdays. His son says today: 'Sybil did not entirely approve as she didn't like his being out of her sight. "He's gone off with his cronies to the old Garrick," she used to say.'

But it is rare for actors who have strong support to be black-balled. The prejudice in their favour has never died, and nor it should. 'All the world's a stage' – and so is the Garrick Club. Look who we prize among members today, from the seniors like Lord Olivier, Sir John Gielgud, Sir John Clements, Sir Alec Guinness, Raymond Huntley and Sir Richard Attenborough. A glance through the first pages of the alphabetical list of members reveals names like Michael Codron, Tom Conti, Tom Courtenay, Andrew Cruikshank, Denholm Elliott, Frank Finlay, Raymond Francis, and so on.

So long as the Garrick Club continues to enjoy the company of actors – and maybe one day, actresses – its heart will remain sound. It also will always need the company of lawyers – pleasant and amusing lawyers, that is, for lawyers can also make the worst bores. One of the very senior and longest serving members declares today that, overall, lawyers make the best members. 'I get very cross when I hear someone who is studying a list of new candidates on the board say, "Oh no, not more bloody lawyers!"'

We also enjoy a sprinkling of artists and authors, architects and 'media' and medical people, rather more than a sprinkling of publishers, who still tend to cluster round 'the publishers' table' as if undesiring of making the acquaintance of anyone outside the book trade. One or two publishers used to leave the Club to find lunch elsewhere if they discovered that the publishers' table was full. Gerald Rivington tried to break this up by refusing to sit down at this, the only circular table, but he had no followers. Roland Gant was once reduced almost to physical force to drag back into the coffee room a publisher who could not face sitting among non-book people at the long table.

Even literary agents now get into the Garrick, the pioneer being the late Peter Watt – 'because he's such a nice and amusing man'. And so he was.

There have always been journalists and Fleet Street tycoons about the place, too, not invariably with happy results, as described elsewhere. They are mostly amusing and well-informed people, too, who add a special element to the Garrick not found elsewhere except in their own exclusive watering holes. Since 1831 they have contributed to 90% of the 'leaks', mostly harmless but some of them embarrassing and damaging. And doubtless so they always will. Fleet Street people, with some honourable exceptions, also tend to be 'cliquey', like bookmen, creating a little club within the Club, and to bring in as guests politicians of every rank and political persuasion and senior civil servants, not one of whom would ever find his name in the candidates' books. This would not have been tolerated twenty-five years ago.

The conduct of business is and always has been prohibited at the Garrick, which is essentially a social club. Satters remembers how, early in his long period as secretary, he saw a member who was lunching a guest producing a stack of papers and placing them on the table. 'I was sitting next to Rivington [Senior Trustee] at the long table and I said, "I know that member is a friend of yours, sir, but if you weren't here I would go across and tell him he really mustn't do that." At once Rivington said, "You go and do it." So I went over and said, "Excuse me, sir, you are breaking one of the rules of the Club." He said something rude but put the papers away. Next day when I came into the bar the member was talking to the chairman. When he saw me he said, "There's the secretary – the bloody man ticked me off for doing business in the Club."

'The Clandestine Marriage'
(Oil by John Zoffany R A)

Charles Mathews as Somno
(Oil by Samuel de Wilde)

Ellen Terry
(Drawing)

Mrs Siddons
(Drawing by Sir Thomas Lawrence PRA)

Peg Woffington
(Oil by Philip Mercier)

Henry Irving
(Oil by Sir John Millais PRA)

'Lock and Key'
(Oil by George Clint ARA)

Marie Tempest
(Oil by J.E. Blanche)

Rivington replied, "He was quite right – come and have a drink." '

I recall seeing a pair of overseas guests from a club with which the Garrick has reciprocal arrangements, lunching together with a large tape recorder on the table. Appraised of this scandal, in came Satters and sternly warned them of the impropriety. Smiling apologetically, they put it under the table, and in fear that it might not be recording audibly, took out their notebooks, scribbling away through the fish course.

There is now, and doubtless there always will be, a sprinkling of rich, influential businessmen members who take absolutely no part in the social 'clubbable' life of the Garrick and contrive to be elected for the sole purpose of entertaining and impressing their business cronies in the unique and impressive ambience of the Club. And, it might be added, at half the cost of a meal at an expense account West End restaurant. The present Trustee and chairman of the general Committee, 'Nunc' Willcox, recalls recently seeing a member dining apart at the long table and approaching him. 'Wouldn't you like to join us?' And so he did, and at the end of a prolonged meal, coffee and liqueurs, remarked, 'I had never realised the Garrick was such a jolly place.' It was the first time in twenty years' membership he had come into the Club without business guests to entertain.

On the other hand the revenue this new trend of business entertaining has attracted has eased the Club's finances to the eventual benefit of the vast majority of members who enjoy the Garrick for the special quality of life there, to which Sir Melford Stevenson has referred: conversation of an amusing nature, the exchange of ideas and news among people who wear their experience and knowledge lightly and are as disposed to listen as to talk, all in an easy-going and friendly atmosphere; with the final bonus of a most agreeable, helpful and often amusing staff, and being always surrounded by numerous, beautiful, well-hung pictures.

The craving for this kind of club life is reflected in the ever-growing list of candidates, now in near-mammoth proportions. The Garrick is, indeed, in very much the condition in which it was placed in the late 1850s: amusing, flourishing, happy, but suffering under the press of numbers by its own popularity. But this time the solution is not to be found in new premises down the road and a dramatic increase in numbers. Some of the early Garrick Club's pleasures were lost in the 1864 move and enlargement, and it is easy to understand the dismay of some members who had to be almost frog-marched from the familiar cosiness of King Street to the wide open spaces of Mr Marrable's Italianite barn. One hundred and twenty years later it would be heresy to deny that small is beautiful, that the limit has been reached, and that 'We are a merry family, We are . . .'

5

Staff

*'The stone that is rolling can gather no moss.
For master and servant, oft changing is loss.'*
Housewifely admonition

EVEN THE OLDEST, crustiest member today will affirm that the Garrick has never before enjoyed a better or happier staff. The reason for this is good management and a perceptive, discriminating judgement for the special qualities that the Garrick needs. Then there is continuity. Only a dozen or so years ago the turnover of staff was so high that, except for the steady stalwarts, the real veterans, you had to give your name, even spell it out, when ordering from the menu. It is equally pleasant to address, and be addressed by, a member of the staff by name as it is to be known by name by your fellow members. Who wrote of 'an ambience of compatability' as a first necessity for a good club?

Today a member has no excuse for failing to remember the face and name of almost every member of the staff. After all, some have been here for more years than the age of younger members. Staff remain at the Club today because there is a first class and understanding secretary, a hostel, good conditions of work and good quarters, and an attractive pension scheme.

The hostel was the brain child of Sir Anthony Burney, to whom the Garrick owes more than a computer can compute, energetically supported by that irreplaceable piece of Garrick treasure, Freddy Lloyd. It is a freehold house in West Kensington with a caretaker in a flat and accommodation for ten members of the staff with their own rooms, two bathrooms, and laundry room. Food is provided at the Club anyway, but for those who wish to cook for themselves at the hostel, there is a well laid out and equipped kitchen. It costs staff – in 1985 – £16 a week, which includes lighting and heating. An office working girl in London would pay twice as much and consider it a bargain. 'It is,' reports the secretary, 'a total success'.

What could be a happier overture to dinner at the Club in the 1980s than Cyril Langley's happy welcome from the lodge, as eager to take a lady's coat as to address her by name, even if he has not seen her for six months. Or, at lunch, Keith Harrison and Barry Watson: 'How are you, sir? Not much of a morning.'

The first member of the staff to greet a member in the hall at lunchtime is quite likely to be Peter Ellick, wine butler, born in St Helena, employed as a waiter at the Travellers until wooed away by Commander Satterthwaite in 1959. Revealing an early talent for recognising quality in wine, Peter was sent for three extended periods of instruction to French vineyards in Champagne, Burgundy and Bordeaux, speaking only French, and only about wine. Today he is as good as any médallion-dangling *buveur* in the depth and extent of his wine knowledge, an unobtrusive guide for those who are not sure but don't want to show it, and more than a match for that absurdly privileged quango, the Garrick Wine Committee.

Tall and erect, somewhat grave in countenance until he greets a member by name, Peter will be on his way to check the wine at a private dinner in the small dining room, the back room or a more formidable occasion in the A.A. Milne Room. There is no greater pleasure in Peter's professional life than discussing the wine to match the menu a member is working out with the chef.

Sydney Powell has for long reigned supreme as head wine waiter, his memories of bibulous members going back thirty years. Wise in his guidance, swift in delivery, sardonic in riposte when this is called for, extensive in his memory of a face or an occasion, Sydney has been described as 'a glorious institution within an institution'. Sydney's is a profession requiring restraint and patience, especially when the 2 o'clock 'fourteen hundred' mob come roaring down from the bar and it has been a hectic lunch for all the staff since 1 o'clock. Anyone who doesn't feel ashamed after stretching Sydney's tolerance to the point of mild rebuke doesn't deserve a drink and has probably had too many already.

Two members sharing a domestic dinner with their wives agreed in turn to buy a bottle of wine, red and white. 'I would like you to find me a bottle of white wine, Sydney, to go with the hors d'oeuvre, quite nice, to show that I'm not stingy.' Second member: 'And, Sydney, for the red, will you pick me out a claret more expensive than the white, but not much more.' Sydney nodded, his head characteristically tilted to indicate complete understanding. At the end of the evening and under the smiling distant gaze of Sydney, a glance at the wine list showed a gap of 5p between the price of the extraordinarily good claret over the excellent chablis.

Today, and for many years past, Mary Williams has officiated in the coffee room and its satellites, a bustling, eager-to-smile figure who contrives to carry as many menus in one hand as Sydney Powell can convey glasses. Queen among waitresses is Jean Peake, whose smile is worth waiting for, her kindness and thoughtfulness beyond compare. Jean has a capacity unique among waitresses of appearing to know what you are going to order before you do so and with a memory for names and faces better than a monarch's equerry. For five terrible years – for the Garrick – Jean disappeared from the coffee room altogether; great was the joy and relief when she returned after having a daughter and setting her on the way from infancy to childhood.

Moira Eagan has been with the Garrick as a nippy, tireless and ever-cheerful waitress for more than a decade, and other long-serving waitresses who put up uncomplainingly with the hesitations, delays and changes of mind of members include Kate Hibbert and Bridget Eivers.

An emperor among bar-keepers is Tony Wilds whose tenure of office goes back to the pre-bar period. Tony will tell of the days when a member ordered a drink by pulling or pushing a bell, like a gentleman in his own home. He will also tell of the days when there were scarcely five hundred members and he knew the names of all of them, and the preferred drink of most of them. In those less hectic days back in the '50s, Tony doubled up as social secretary and barman, dispensing drinks and introductions for new members simultaneously. 'It was,' recalls one veteran member, 'a spectacular piece of juggling'. Today, such is the press of numbers in the bar before lunch that it is all he, and his assistant, the amiable Peter Gormley, can do to keep pace with importunate members elbowing their way forward, an ingratiating or desperate smile on their face.

Tony, chunky of figure and modest in stature, has an elephantine memory, which he displays casually as if this was a shared rather than an exclusive gift. A one-time member who had not been in Tony's bar for five years arrived as a guest in the throes of the 1.15 pm mob rule. His special drink was at once placed on the bar by Tony, smiling a welcome, his voice just audible through the decibels of egomania: 'How nice to see you, sir'. At quieter times in the evening, Tony practises another double act of chatting to one or a group of members while keeping a swivelling eye open for new arrivals and their needs.

'What is the first thing you notice about Tony?' 'Equability.' 'And next?' 'His dry martinis and bloody marys.' But it is not long before his kindness and thoughtfulness enter the conversation as the praises are sung to this peerless bartender. 'I really don't know what we are going to do when Tony finally goes,' remarked one of the Trustees recently in the deepest gloom. 'He's almost impossible to replace.' Tony is a great reader and generous authors give him a copy of their latest book. He can be of material help to an author, too, particularly to thriller writers, for he is a real authority on guns and ballistics.

There are a number of lovable and some quaint figures to be found in staff history. One of the first staff demanded by Commander Satterthwaite was a carpenter-cum-fire man – 'I must have someone to do the fires, it's a full-time job in winter.' Thus there entered into the staff quarters in 1953 the enigmatic figure of Mr F. G. Timms. His work was faultless: the grates shone, the fires blazed and all his little jobs were completed promptly and efficiently. But he never spoke, except to acknowledge a request from the secretary. He never uttered a word for over five years, until at length he became accepted as the silent handyman in blue overalls with a scuttle of coal in each hand. Then one day a member of the staff invited him to play a game of billiards. At the green baize he became a transformed figure, chattering away enthusiastically about wrinkles and tactics, and displaying an exceptional skill which could have been explained only by his spending every moment of his free time in some billiards saloon.

More recently there was an Irish cleaner called Pat Mullett. He did not talk very much either, but he could not play billiards. His forté, it was eventually learned, was ballroom dancing, in some premises in south London. He lived in the Club, and one day, just before lunch, he died in the Club. After a great deal of trouble taken by the secretary, and by the *gardai* of the Republic of Ireland, two unmarried sisters, his only relatives, were discovered in a remote village. They came to London for the first time in their lives, cleared the pathetically few possessions of their brother, and departed. The room was still full of rubbish, however, and the Secretary ordered it to be cleaned out – 'everything – absolutely everything'. A final inspection of the cleared and cleaned room revealed some neatly folded newspapers in a bottom drawer. Beneath them the secretary found no fewer than seventy weekly wage packets, each carefully slit open to extract the loose change for evenings out at the ballroom, but otherwise intact. £2,700 was despatched to the sisters in their remote Irish village.

In the Garrick bar amongst the portraits of actors and actresses, distinguished men of letters and the law, there is a full-length Jack Gilroy (1955) portrait of Freddy Barker in characteristic pose, a tray bearing a bottle and glass in his left hand. Barker, ever full of grave goodwill and malapropisms, presided over the wine in the coffee room for many years and latterly, when less nippy on his legs, dispensed drinks in the lounge. Barker was, at once, a figure who attracted much affection and was the Garrick butt who found himself innocently lured into comment on matters relating to the Club and to the wider world beyond the barn. Commander Satterthwaite recalls: 'I had not been in the Club many months when some member quite improperly asked Barker what he thought of the new secretary. The reply was, "If I may say so, sir, he is absolutely identical." '

[87]

Shortly before the 1964 General Election, and after lunch when spirits and feelings were running freely in the lounge, Barker was asked how he was going to vote. 'Oh, for the socialists, sir,' deferentially placing a brimming glass of madeira before his questioner. 'For the socialists, Barker? I am astonished at you.' Barker, retrieving an empty glass: 'Oh, sir, I would not presume to vote with the members.'

After a number of members had been watching on television the state carriage delivering the Queen to the Palace of Westminster, one turned to Barker who had been watching discreetly at the door. 'What did you like best about it, Barker?' 'Oh, it was *lovely*, sir. It was the indignity of it I liked best.'

Tom Girtin tells of the overseas member making his first visit to the Club for a number of years, delighted to be greeted by name by the hall porter. Barker opened the glass door at the top of the steps to him, also greeting him by name. Delighted and flattered, the overseas member asked, 'Tell me, Barker, how is it that you and the porter manage to remember the names of members you haven't seen for years?' Barker replied smartly, 'Well, sir, you see we try and pick on some redeeming feature.' Girtin also believes that 'while relishing this I would like to think that Barker knew exactly what he was saying, that he knew exactly how to be a Character and that, contrary to the overseas member's belief, Barker was speaking no less than the truth'. It is possible – some believe even likely – that with the example of so many actors and advocates all about him every day for so many years, he felt the need to play a part of his own, that of staff wag. If so, it was a wonderfully accomplished, solemn and consistent performance. All the world is, indeed, a stage. He might not presume to vote with the members but he could well have not felt the same reluctance to act with the members.

A club is only as good as its members, it used to be said; it must be added in these more enlightened times: and its staff. When the

[88]

club is happy and flourishing, so are the staff; and vice versa. Whenever the club is going through a bad patch, almost invariably there is staff trouble.

'The year of the move' from King Street to the new clubhouse was a very unhappy time, with terrible bickering and hurled abuse among members whose roots were being wrenched from the heart of Covent Garden to some terrible Italianite barn. Amidst all this hurly-burly, and no doubt taking advantage of it, two coffee room waiters absconded with £41 13s 2d. Money had rather rashly been left with one of them for the convenience of members to change cheques; the other 'was unable to pay the amount due to the steward for dinner bills received'. They left, under a cloud, for the police to pick up, and were deprived of their contributions to the staff fund. Their names were Thomas Crook and Alfred Light. Light had been superintendent of the coffee room since 1858, at £50 pa, apparently not enough.

In earlier days there was more staff trouble, especially in the kitchen, reflecting disturbance 'upstairs'. The Club's finances were poor in 1837–8 and giving cause for concern. Economies were imposed. 'It is ordered that the lamps in the reading room be put out at 12 o'clock, the two-light chandelier to be discontinued, and the French lamps placed on the table.' And 'that the Courier des Théâtres be discontinued'.

When these economies extended to the kitchen, there were protests. The highly reputed cook quickly gave way to one Thompson. Thompson was soon given a month's notice. 'A female cook should be employed instead of a man,' it was decided. Cheaper. And so it came about that 'Melbourn presented herself before the Committee and was engaged as Cook provided her character was approved, her wages to be 30 guineas a year, including washing'. References were taken up with the Blenheim Hotel, Bond Street, and found to be satisfactory. She did not last long, and by June 1839, barely six months later, her successor, Mrs Jones, 'was to be discharged on Monday morning next'. Next came Lefure, 'recommended by Morel of 210 Piccadilly'; and so it was back to more expensive (£50 a year) men.

Within days, Lefure was causing concern: 'Resolved, that the Cook be admonished by the Secretary for leaving the House all night without permission.' By December, he had gone and there may well have been others in between. 'Several cooks were seen by the Committee,' we read, 'when Duport the assistant cook of the Junior United Services Club was engaged at 60 guineas a year without any perquisite whatever'.

Dishonesty as well as slackness among the staff when the club's finances are weak and the climate is generally unhappy occur too often among the Club's records to be coincidental. During these same difficult times, there are several references to petty purloining. 'James Jiggins, Steward, takes every day 1s more than he accounts for . . . He is in the constant habit of making two bills for each person, one of which he destroys . . . He will not let [Ellen Byron, cashier] receive the amount of the bills from the waiters but takes it himself and puts it in his pocket . . . He has staid out all night.'

'What's the matter now at the Garrick Club?' a correspondent enquired a hundred years ago, at the time of another Garrick black period. 'The butler and all the staff of waiters are leaving, because, as they say, the pay is altogether out of proportion to the amount of work they are expected to do. It may be added that no club servants in London are so hardly worked as those at the Garrick.' Readers of this scandalous item were then told that the Club was quite rich enough 'to enable this reproach to be removed forthwith' and that the whole matter was likely to be warmly discussed at the next Committee meeting. 'As fast as new waiters come in they leave, even to the point of forfeiting their wages,' and the staff's food was apparently inedible.

No doubt there was not much paternalism, or even politeness, under these conditions. It has never been good form to be rude to Club staff. Today the worst thing that can be said of a member is, 'He's damn rude to the servants'. Quite right, too. Recently an otherwise amusing and popular member suffered from this failing when in his cups, and after a particularly unhappy episode felt obliged to resign.

[90]

The presence of good staff is a priceless asset, and most old members, before they hang up their hideous cucumber and salmon tie for the last time, recall with equal warmth their happy relationship with the Garrick staff as with fellow members. It was once quite common for members to leave a bequest, usually of one hundred guineas, to the staff fund along with an appreciative note just as he might show his gratitude to his butler, valet, coachman and cook. This old practice could usefully be revived.

The crisis in staff relations in the 1880s and the adverse publicity this aroused left its mark, and a tradition of care and welfare and (relative) generosity has been maintained for a long time now. A Staff Provident Fund was established in 1922, to which the staff contributed, with supplementary contributions from Club funds and the Christmas Box Fund. We read of Mr M.S. Grenet, the chef for twenty years after his appointment in 1911 ('with four years away in the trenches') on his retirement being given a pension of £30 a year; while Mrs Nichols, a charwoman from 1915 to 1931, being offered £10 from the fund and a pension for life of 7s 6d a week.[1] Then Miss G. Pockney was granted £78 19s 2d from the staff fund with a pension of £1 a week for 12 months, to be reviewed 'provided that she did not take employment in the meantime'. Miss Draper, at the same time (July 1931) did not, it seems, qualify for a pension but was given a gift of £5 and a grant from the fund of £79 7s 2d. The club finances at this time, in the depression, were not healthy.

Later, at the height of another crisis in the summer of 1940, the general Committee approved a pension of £2 a week for Mr W. Brown (20 years service) with a grant from the fund of £172 0s 10d.[2] At the next monthly meeting, June 1940, a resolution was proposed that staff who volunteered for service in the armed forces should be granted their share from the pension fund. Several Committee members opposed this and suggested that only members of the staff 'who are called up for compulsory military or civilian service' should be so privileged. This resolution was passed, which seems a curious anomaly. Quite reasonably, the staff thought so, too, and rejected the whole unpatriotic idea. Why should those who volunteered be penalized while those conscripted benefit? The Committee were forced to reconsider, with the result that Mr B. Last received £31 8s 10d on joining the colours (pay 2s a day) and Mr H.Evans was presented with £31 8s 10d cash, less £6 owing for an unpaid loan.[3]

Twenty-five years earlier the First World War had brought its own staff problems, especially after Lord Kitchener had opened his massive recruitment drive. For the first time waitresses were admitted to the coffee room, to the dismay of some, and especially old, members. But at the end of hostilities, a newspaper cutting tells us, 'There is a possibility that the Garrick Club may discard waitresses altogether.' The same correspondent believed 'that a well-backed resolution to that effect comes up at the next annual meeting'.[4] It did not. (More inaccurate tittle-tattle about the Garrick appears in the newspapers than about any other national institution except the Palace.)

The Second World War brought with it even more serious staff shortages. Before the 1940 bombing of London it was a shortage of members that seriously preoccupied the general Committee. This was solved as a result of the bombing of the Beefsteak, the Travellers and the Fly-Fishers, all of which sought, and received, hospitality in Garrick Street. But now the sheer weight of numbers led to a falling off in service, exacerbated by the Minister of Labour, Ernest Bevin, who tightened the labour market, putting most waiters and waitresses above conscription age into factories. Cynics noted that Bevin himself was elected a member unanimously under Rule 15 in January 1941, but even this did not help matters.

Eighteen months later all the Beefsteak, Travellers and Fly-Fisher refugees were ready to return home. They did so gratefully, the Fly-Fishers in October 1942 presenting David Garrick's fishing rod to the Club as a token of appreciation.

'The staff quarters were deplorable when I joined,' says Commander Satterthwaite. 'But then so were most of the staff.' The turnover of staff had been horrendous for some years, pay was poor and morale very low. At the coronation day party later in the year, the only people who got drunk were the two wine waiters, found flat on the floor totally unconscious. They had to go, and after they had gone it was discovered that one of them had been fiddling the wine for years; a member recalled being invited to his flat where he was offered very good Garrick wine.

But at least Coleman was there, and the ex-soldier and the ex-sailor got on well from the start. And there were some gems among the dross, like Barker of course, and Sydney, and Jean, a very young and pretty waitress. Then there were Mr and Mrs Peters, she another waitress and he a fine hard-drinking wine butler, who was soon to be understudied appropriately by Peter. Club hall porters, in an ideal world, should never change; they have to know every member's name and preferably his wife's name and often a good deal more. All this knowledge takes time to build up. Old Gunther in 1953 had been in the lodge since the last century, or so it seemed to some members. But he had become very senile and immobile, so Satters had to pension him off with regret. In his place came Bedford, another ex-soldier. He and the new secretary had an unofficial identity contest, one often attempting to beat the other. 'You know who that is, sir?' 'Yes, Bedford, that's His Honour Judge Rowlandson, and with him is Sir Geoffrey Perry.' 'Quite right, sir, just checking.' That sort of thing.

The year 1953 was one of reform and tightening up; Satters came, slackers left; morale improved. By the time of the Club dinner with the Duke of Edinburgh in the chair, the Club's machinery was running more smoothly and it was a happier place downstairs. 'Anne Frost was my assistant,' says Satters today. 'A wonderful woman. She supervised everything. We would walk about the Club together and between us we knew everything that was going on.'

Head waitresses had for long replaced head waiters. Just as the butlers of old had been the key to eating contentment (with the chef), so this responsibility now rested on the shoulders of the head waitress. These tireless women have borne the burden of their considerable duties well over the years, and a number of figures – some of them quite ample – have a place in Garrick history. There was Betty Fortey and Kitty Keyes back in the 1950s and '60s, much loved by all; and Joan Johnson, who could always be relied upon to squeeze in another member or two when there was clearly no room to breathe in at the long table.

Joan was also known to give passing offence to some of the more pompous members who thought servants should keep their distance, and certainly not mildly tease them. Joan used to read her own poetry on the radio, and translated from the Russian. She once composed a poem while presiding in the coffee room. The poem was for two poets and a poetess, Mary Wilson, the wife of the prime minister, Ogden Nash and John Betjeman, all guests of Robert Lusty and his wife. In the course of a very extended dinner, Ogden Nash had composed a self-apologetic poem for Mary Wilson, beginning, 'Diogenes would not admire / The Morals of this versifier / Who became a man of letters / By simply stealing from his betters . . .' Then the entire party, which included a publisher or two, sang the praises of Joan the poetic head waitress, which led her to retire into a corner with a pen and her order pad.⁵ Alas, her contribution has not survived.

Once upon a time there were staff evenings when members of the house committee, in black ties, reversed rôles and served the staff while games, dancing and a good deal of merry drinking went on. Latterly they became less successful in inverse ratio with the onset of egalitarianism until they simply ran out of steam. Today's staff–member relationship would be quite incomprehensible to a between-the-wars member; outrageous to Sir Charles Taylor or Sir Henry Irving. In fact it is just about right for these times, with mutual respect, courtesy and concern, and a total absence of the sort of patronising which passed for 'getting on well with the servants' not so long ago.

When many of us enter the clubhouse today we are as pleased and reassured to see and chat to a smiling member of the staff as of a fellow member. The two experiences provide a subtle amalgam which is the essence of Garrick zest and well-being.

6

Food and Drink

'. . . eating boiled ham and treacle pudding . . .'
CHARLIE CHAPLIN at the Garrick

FOR SOME 150 YEARS the Garrick has prided itself, not always accurately, that its cuisine has been a cut above that of other clubs. Club chefs was the subject of a conversation at the round table at lunch recently, Boodles's food being compared with Brooks's, the Carlton's with the Travellers'. 'What about the Athenaeum's chef?' someone interjected. 'I haven't lunched there for years. Who's the chef?' Roland Gant cried in disbelief. 'Chef? Don't they have Meals-on-Wheels there?'

The reason for the generally but *not* invariably high standard of cuisine at the Garrick is popularly ascribed to the gluttony of the legal profession rather than the traditional discrimination of members associated with the arts. Very aged members have told of indifferent food in the dim past, though Melford Stevenson describes the food in the early '30s as 'excellent and expensive' and Raymond Huntley swears that the food during the Second World War was 'excellent; better than today'. But, at least, from the beginning most members have cared, even if they have occasionally endured ghastly cooking.

From the Club's earliest days it has been the practice (and is so today) to write complaints of a meal on the reverse of the bill; like 'Lamb tastes of oil cake' or 'Only six or eight stale beans served' (1894), or 'Soup made of decomposed hare' (1892).

Things started off quite well at King Street back in 1832. 'The Garrick Club,' revealed a newspaper, 'have wisely engaged in the kitchen the far-famed Soloman of the Piazza Coffee-house. The Committee of noblemen and gentlemen who superintend this establishment have placed the charges for eating and drinking upon the lowest scale.'

Soloman was succeeded by the string of failures and then the woman, Melbourn. 'Much of its nineteenth-century cuisine was managed by a woman cook,' according to Mr Escott, 'one of the few consummate *cordons bleus* then known in the club world'.¹ In spite of this flattering assertion, the Committee minutes reveal the quitting or dismissing of a great many more chefs during the mid-nineteenth century, when they were paid between £100 and £150 pa, and much dissatisfaction with the food. 'The secretary was asked to give the cook one month's notice to leave' (5 November 1864).

'I am sorry to begin my annual campaign against the vegetables,' declares a member (4 June 1859), although I suspect he was relishing writing his complaint once again. 'I paid 1s 6d for twenty-five heads of asparagus today. The finest in the market (I went round to see) were from 4s to 4s 6d a hundred. Those I had were *exceedingly bad*. I then bought some more for myself and for 1s got three dozen much better *very* fresh. I should add that my first dish was served on a bit of toast which would have disgraced the lowest and cheapest cookshop; and which created "a lively reaction" at the table. I sent it down to be looked at by Alfred. (Signed) Albert Smith'

The Committee were clearly hardened to Mr Smith's complaints about Alfred and his ingredients, gave a deep sigh, 'moved, seconded and carried unanimously, that in consequence of the language in which the complaint is made, that no notice be taken of it by the committee'. Quite right, too; it seems to me that he was getting his asparagus dirt cheap.

However, a year later when another member complained that he had eaten better chicken elsewhere, the secretary was instructed 'to enquire from Mr Fisher, Duke Street, St James's, whether he is willing to supply the club on the same terms and with the same quality of poultry as he supplies to the Carlton Club,'² indicating that politeness in the Garrick improves everything, including the chicken, and also that other clubs might have food of a higher quality.

There was, better still, a practice in those days, and for long after, of members presenting provisions to the Club, which then appeared like this: 'Smoked Salmon (by courtesy of His Honour Judge Henry) 2s 6d'. Another pleasant practice that lasted into the 1930s and that could be revived was to serve breakfast at the Garrick, either in 'the visitors' room' or in the coffee room later.

Oysters in season have always been popular at the Garrick; which makes this entry in the minutes more mysterious: 'An offer to supply oysters direct from the sea at Whitstable at 10/- per 100 declined . . .' (1 December 1902)

Following a suggestion to the Committee in February 1888 'it was ordered that in addition to the present hot lunch at 1s/- there should be a hot joint served each week day from 1.30 to 2.30 at the price of 1s/6d each including table money'. Cheap, even for those days. So was this: Luncheon only

Plate of cold meat or chop, with bread only 6d
ditto with potatoes and pickles 1/-
Bread, cheese and butter 6d[3]

But some people (in this case Marshall Hall) are never satisfied:

14 April 1893

Bread & Butter 6d
I cannot understand why I am charged for bread and butter *in addition* to Table Money (8d). I never ordered it but it was brought with the plovers' eggs and I have been charged for butter separately. I may mention also that the brown bread and butter was very bad, having been evidently cut for some time.

Through the Edwardian period everything points to the Garrick serving up good plain fare, well cooked prep school stuff, with the chef excelling and enjoying himself for special occasions, particularly when King Edward himself, Patron and gourmet, came to dinner. Then the menu was printed in French, and a great many members could not understand what they were going to eat, or possibly, had eaten.

As told elsewhere, there were some culinary privations as a result of the U-boats in the First World War, though not all that many.

From an item in the *Evening News* we learn about the eccentric feeding habits of members rather than their privations:

> At the Garrick Club I was much struck by the curious meals taken by actors. Holman Clark and A.E. Matthews were drinking cocoa with meat, concluding with creme de menthe. Granville Barker started quite like ordinary people do, with soup and fish, but then suddenly skidded badly and ordered himself 'Gentleman's Relish' on toast.[4]

Harley Granville-Barker was at that time working at the War Office in the same Special Intelligence department as a fellow Garrick member and friend (and also Clara Butt's husband) Kennerley Rumford. They both loved an excuse for holding a dinner at the Garrick, when 'Rumford is very generous, and thinks nothing of singing five or six songs to his delighted audience'.

A generally high standard, for clubs, was maintained through the 1920s and 1930s, and the surviving menus for special occasions reflect at least a very elaborate choice. For a decade or more after the Second World War, Coleman presided. Coleman could be brilliant when he wanted to, especially for the Club dinner and the Derby, and awful if he disapproved. The Spanish Ambassador, a diplomatic member, ordered paella and a Spanish omelette, a quite reasonable request under the circumstances you would suppose, but Judge Billy Hughes, who witnessed the occasion, saw Coleman's face fall with horror. 'It was absolutely ghastly,' recalls Billy. 'But when another member complained to Coleman the next day he was not in the least contrite. "Ask for rubbish, you'll get rubbish!"'

Meat rationing was still applying when Coleman arrived, which tested his skills straightaway. Coleman's, and Satters's, first Club dinner was a challenge, for the Duke of Edinburgh, now the Patron, was guest of honour. Satters thought he should get to Buckingham Palace to find out what H.R.H. liked to eat. He was told he only liked steak. 'What chance of a hundred steaks?' the secretary asked the Club supplier. 'None at all,' he was told crisply. So Satters asked around and eventually settled on Russells of

Smithfield Market. 'A hundred steaks, sir? No trouble at all.' So Satters told Russells he would transfer the Club's custom and they would keep it for as long as they gave complete satisfaction. They did so, for many years. And Coleman produced one hundred tenderly grilled steaks for the Club dinner, and much else that was – so it was said – stunningly successful.

Coleman was the last of the individualist chefs – in more than one sense. 'In those days,' Satters recalls, 'we had around fifty for lunch, and perhaps twenty for dinner on average'. A chef could give individual attention to each dish. 'Now,' says the present secretary, 'it is very difficult because you have two different types of member, the *haute cuisine* and the indifferent. And now we have to cope with two hundred covers a day. Coleman could do everything himself. Now we have two *sous chefs*.'

One reason for the great increase in the number of meals served at the Garrick – apart from the parties and special dinners – is the grill room after-theatre supper. This 1970s revival was not the first. Late suppers at the Garrick have come and gone again with the frequency of chefs, and perhaps because of them, for there is *nothing* so depressing as a dreary meal at midnight. Here is evidence of one revival, 19 May 1882:

Resolved

That, in accordance with the recommendation of the Special Committee, suppers be served to members and visitors in the Strangers Dining Room from 10.30 p.m. until 1.30 a.m. *and that the room be closed at 1.30 a.m.*

That members be allowed to introduce not more than two friends between the above named hours.

In February 1976 the Garrick was dead by 10 pm. Then, suddenly, you could drop in after the play or opera at any time up to midnight, at first without booking. The menu was shorter than for dinner but perfectly adequate, and in spite of forebodings by some it was a howling success from the start: a lot more revenue, and a lot more late night fun, bringing back some of the old Victorian spirit.

[99]

The skills practised in the kitchens today are as fine as they have ever been, and Stephen Lattimer, the chef, can and does prepare meals as good as any old greedy barrister of the 1880s ever enjoyed. But with all the pressure of increased numbers, the menu is necessarily more restricted than it has sometimes been and the need to make use of modern short-cuts and aids has led to a tendency towards institutional food, albeit of a high standard.

No such compromise has been called for in the drinks department. There is something timeless about drinks at the Garrick, an impression created in part by the continuing high standard of the wines and the rewarding and informed manner in which drinks are served by stewards and wine waiters who appear to all but the oldest members to have never changed. You have to have been a member for well over thirty years to have pre-dated Tony, and Peter the wine steward should be wearing almost as many long-service decorations. Anyone with membership of more than ten years will remember the wine waiter Freddy Barker, a seemingly ageless figure, too, who gave his whole life to the Garrick and was deeply loved in return. Barker originally served under the mighty figure of Dunn, who went back to the middle ages and could tell tales of Henry Irving and served brandy and sodas when founder members like 'Papa' Fladgate were still alive.

Of this Methuselah of a wine waiter, Melford Stevenson recalls today: 'At the end of an evening Dunn would clear all the liqueur glasses, pouring the dregs into a pint pot – armagnac, green chartreuse, brandy, madeira – and then drink down the lot. He had the most expensive complexion I have ever seen. I used to sit beside him on the last number 11 bus around midnight and he would tell me tales of members from way back. Dunn was so universally respected that some members, like Seymour Hicks, would always call him Mr Dunn.'

It was as well that old Mr Dunn had a bus to take him home. There was a tragic case recently of a member driving home after a long dinner and killing himself. Not so the one-time Recorder at Maidstone, Reggie Seaton. He would come into the club at around 10 pm and drink whisky steadily and not slowly until 2 am. Then he would drive himself back to Maidstone. Satters once cautioned him about the dangers of this, but he took no notice and never had an accident. 'Oh yes, he did,' Satters corrects himself. 'He had two accidents, both of them in his own drive, hitting a tree. The same tree.'

Dunn was a wine and liqueur man and despised cocktails. This led to complaints among some of the younger, more raffish members, and in April 1930, in an effort to correct the low standard of sidecars and other vulgar mixes, it was decreed that 'a servant should be sent to the Savoy Hotel and shown how to make cocktails': surely the only shameful blot on the Garrick's drinking history.

Incidentally at the same meeting at which this decision was made, we can read the following item, typical of committee meetings until quite recent years when the wine committee remains sphinx-like about what it buys for us after its intensive and prolonged tastings.

> Purchased Clicquot '23
> 3 doz magnums @ 298/-
> 25 doz bottles @ 144/-
> 30 doz pints @ 77/-

A cocktail might be considered only for 'the fast set', but punch was something else, and always respectable, particularly at summer parties. The Garrick gin-punch goes back into the heavy alcoholic haze of Garrick history, certainly to King Street. This in 1855:

> The Garrick is noted for its summer gin-punch, thus made: Pour half a pint of gin on the outer peel of a lemon, then a little lemon-juice, a glass of maraschino, a pint and a quarter of water and two bottles of iced soda water.[5]

'Inspiration has been quickened by the famous Gin Punch,' Fitzgerald recalled, '– a special recipe dear to Theodore Hook, and on which I have heard "Boz" expatiate in heartiest praise. "Try that gin-punch he would say, and then see!"' It is good to know one *could* see.

[101]

When the Marlborough Club, after amalgamating with Wyndham's, finally packed up in the 1950s the Garrick, suspecting that there might be rich seams in the wine cellars, the wine committee took the secretary along. Quick thinking, instant action, paid a handsome dividend. The Garrick bought the lot – and the barman and the cellarman who had looked after it, as a bonus. This was how the Club acquired Tony Wilds and 'Nobby' Clark, a great Garrick wine figure and assistant barman for many years.

The cellarage at King Street being so restricted, the Club relied on immediate deliveries from its wine merchants with a small store in a cupboard. Matters soon improved, however, but there was never adequate space for the storage of wine in the old building, this being one of the many factors that led to the Committee recommending a change of premises. Substantial cellarage was included in Mr Marrable's plans for the new Club house but with the increase in number of members, and perhaps their consumption, these cellars had to be enlarged.

> Your Committee [Wine, 15 March 1884] have made a careful personal examination of the existing limited cellar accommodation and the capacity of the building for storing additional wine. The only feasible course seems to be the removal of china and glass cupboards now placed in the wide passage leading to the coal cellar, and placing bins in their stead.
>
> This would provide room for about 1,000 dozen which your Committee think would give separate and sufficient cellarage to the two merchants now supplying the Club.

Sir George Armytage of the wine committee who signed this recommendation would be impressed by the state and capacity of the Garrick wine cellars today, where there is room for 35,000 bottles, or around $3\frac{1}{2}$ cases per member. This stock has been built up over the years from numerous wine merchants. Today there are six main suppliers, although small quantities – a case or two – are obtained from many other wine merchants clamouring for the Club's custom.

As for the table wines, these were literally available on the tables *en carafe* until the early 1970s, members recording the number of glasses drunk to the cashier. But sometimes some members with poor memories underestimated their consumption – a sad fact first reported in February 1972. Because at that time the Club's excess of expenditure over income was about £24,000 something had to be done: the welcome-looking carafes were removed, and since then the ever busy wine waiters have had to do all the work.

A brief glance down memory lane to Bordeaux:

19 March 1900: Considered question of purchase of a little fine Claret. Samples to be procured of:
Mouton-Rothschild 1868 @ 100/-
Lafite 1868 @ 90/-
Lafite 1878 @ 117/-

A sad note on the generally happy subject of drinking:

3 October 1887:
The following club wines found to be ullaged, or with blown corks, at the quarterly stock-taking were ordered to be written off the stock viz.

	£	s	d
2 magnums Lanson 19/-	1	18	0
3 bottles do 10/-	1	10	0
2¼ galls: S. Whisky 27/-	3	0	9

and nine more items.

But, to end on a happier note: it seems that Covent Garden porters' carts, always crowding the streets before the market left for another site some years ago, were often parked in doorways, including the Garrick's doorway, obliging late-nighters to return inside for just one more for the road while it was cleared. But on 23 June 1890 the Committee decided this had gone too far. 'Complaint having been made of the obstruction caused at night by empty carts blocking the entrance, the Secretary was requested to write to the police authorities.'

7

Skits and Sketches

Sketch: *'A short play or performance of slight dramatic
construction and usually of a light or comic nature.'* O.E.D.

A NEW MEMBER'S first 'solo' visit to the Garrick has either been
lost in the alcoholic cloud which blotted out the experience, or is
recalled with vivid clarity, sometimes of an uncomfortable nature.
When there were only four hundred or so members, a new member
was rapidly picked out, and always made welcome. Today it is
much more difficult and the initiative, alas, often lies with the new
member himself. I recall the late John Vaizey (1973) making his
first solo and without any pushiness at all becoming absorbed into
a group at the bar and contributing his characteristic sardonic wit.
Others have not been so lucky, or their nerve has failed them and
they have made their way from the bar into lunch instead. They
should have been reassured that they would have been welcomed
into any group of chatterers.

'The mere mention of the Garrick Club,' wrote Squire Bancroft
in 1909 (elected 1869) 'recalls great happiness enjoyed within its
walls for forty years. I was received there in my youth with a
welcome never to be forgotten, by men of mark in all the walks
of life . . .'[1]

Another squire, 'the squire of Piccadilly' as he liked to be called,
otherwise William Stone, also received a warm welcome. 'The
first time I went, very diffidently, into the Garrick Club, sixty-two
years ago, an old man, Walter Lacy, who must have been one of
the handsomest men in London – he was *jeune premier* to the great
Macready at Drury Lane – stood up and gravely bowed. "I think,"
he said, "I have the honour of welcoming a new member".'[2]

About a century later author–publisher Roland Gant recalls his
first solo with some discomfiture. 'I was wearing a dog-tooth suit
and a bow tie, and feeling fearfully shy as I walked tentatively into

the coffee room. *Everybody* was talking at the tops of their voices, as usual, and there was only one seat left – and at the head of the long table at that. I had already turned to disappear ignominiously when an aged member called out, "Seat there, seat there, come and sit down". I did so, and the same old man asked me, "You're a new member aren't you?" I admitted this. "And what have I seen you in recently?" "Nothing, sir." "Resting, eh?" Before I could explain that I was only an editor, another voice boomed out, far down the table. It was Donald Wolfit, raising his leonine head and staring in my direction. "Don't tell me we've elected *another* actor member." By this time I was nearly in tears . . .'

The late James Mason, a real actor, recalled his first solo as an uncomfortable experience, too. 'Shortly after I was made a member I decided suddenly to go in for dinner one evening. The coffee room was empty so I sat down with a paper and began reading it, hoping that someone would soon turn up. The waitress did, and asked me to put my paper away as it was contrary to custom. Feeling an ass I did so. After a long interval some other members drifted in, took one look in my direction and sat elsewhere. I hope it was because my face is quite well known and people were shy of appearing "pushy" by sitting near me. But it wasn't until there was nowhere else to sit that I got a neighbour. And then it was fine and everybody was very nice and I had a lovely evening.'

A very much older member than Roland Gant, or James Mason, was told when he was much younger by an old member that before the First World War the coffee room had a line of single tables under the window at which members sat, *with their hats on*, reading the *Pall Mall Gazette* or *The Nineteenth Century*. The hats were 'to emphasise the fact that it was a members' club, with each member owning a fraction of it'.[3] The hats went, probably with the war, but single tables remained well into the 1920s. This is Duff Cooper in 1919: 'I dined last night at the Garrick and read Chambonas [Compte A. de la Garde-Chambonas] on the Congress of Vienna – a charming book well worth reading.'[4] Try to imagine that scene today!

But it appears the future Lord Norwich did sometimes talk to other members: 'I have seconded old Denison Ross for the Garrick Club – the election is today – one has to write a letter to the Committee saying what you know of the candidate. I couldn't think of anything to say of Ross except that he was England's greatest orientalist. [A.E.W.] Mason came up to me last night and said "Can't you say something else about him – half the old fools on the Committee don't know what an 'orientalist' is – they'll probably think you mean he's a bugger." '⁵ Well, Hugh Walpole had proposed him and Somerset Maugham supported the orientalist, too. But he got in all right.

The Garrick Tie: you might think that two apocryphal stories about its origins would be, perhaps, more than enough. There are at least half a dozen. These two will do.

Sir Gerald du Maurier was walking with a friend along Jermyn Street and they stopped outside a haberdasher's shop. In the window was a pink and green tie. The friend said, 'I bet you wouldn't dare wear that tie in the Garrick, Gerald.' 'A fiver?' 'Done.' He changed ties and as he entered the Garrick, he was greeted 'Good God, Gerald, what's that ghastly tie.' 'It's the Garrick tie.' And it was.

Another story has it that Seymour Hicks and drunken friends decided at the end of lunch that the Garrick should have a tie, and made off into the Strand where, in the Savoy Tailors' Guild, they fingered through a great many until Hicks exclaimed, 'My favourite dish! Salmon and cucumber!'

Garrick members are very funny about the Club tie. They affect to despise it and yet always wear it on television. Even non-members have been seen on the box wearing it, which I suppose is a sort of tribute, if cheeky. I confess to a weakness for flaunting it in the pavilion at Lords, if only to show that there is such a thing as an equally hideous club tie to the M.C.C.'s. In June 1984 at a garden party the Club Patron, Prince Philip, saw a member wearing a new, *clean* Garrick tie. 'That's not a *real* Garrick tie,' protested Prince Philip. 'But it is, sir,' affirmed the member. 'Oh no, it's not,' argued H.R.H., 'there are no gravy stains'. Members appear to pour their soup down their club ties, perhaps for the same reason – to demonstrate how veteran they are – as R.A.F. pilots poured beer over their caps, then engine oil.

There is a sad tie story about the late and very long-serving member, Sir William Walton. He married in mid-life 'an energetic lady from Argentina' named Susana Gil Paso, after half a lifetime of bachelorhood. Soon after this event he could not find his Garrick tie and asked Susana, who told him 'Oh, that old thing – I threw it away.' Worse still, it had once belonged to his friend and mentor, Sir Edward Elgar.

In spite of Roland Gant's dog-tooth suit, *outrée* clothes are not much to be seen around the Garrick these days. We could do with a few more eccentric members in wide-brimmed hats and silk neck ties, someone like Claude Lowther. He came in once 'dressed in a very flamboyant fashion, with a satin-lined cloak, diamonds and so forth. "Dear me," said a member from the lounge, "Who are you?" And when he was informed that the name was Claude Lowther, "What I would call you is a bloody loud clothier".'[6]

Another quaint dresser, not even a member, was treated more courteously, as Max Reinhardt recalls:

It was about 1.30 and the Coffee Room was full as usual, and bubbling with activity. So much so, that hardly anybody noticed at first the man who walked into the room in a dark suit with a cloak around him, wearing a hat *à la gondoliérè* without the ribbon. He came through the Coffee Room door and walked to the mantelpiece, dropped his bag and started reciting Shakespeare. Suddenly there was silence because I saw the secretary coming in to the room and he must have asked the servants to stop any activity.

The stranger then complained that the working actors, and particularly the Garrick, did not pay enough attention to the unemployed actors, and started looking for something in his bag. I thought he was going to produce a gun. The conversation started again, louder than before, and the poor fellow could hardly be heard. It was a truly marvellous scene of which the Garrick members could well be proud. I think he would have gone on for a very long time, but was stopped by a policeman. No-one referred to the incident for a while until we all started being a little curious and asking each other if they had heard what he had said or if he had been a former member who had been asked to resign. It ended by being quite an enjoyable occasion and I think some extra champagne flowed as a result.

A dip back into the last century, courtesy of Percy Fitzgerald, and mainly booksy:

We find a very cruel attack on 'Boz's' biographer, John Forster, whose unfortunate manner, seems to have made him hosts of enemies. 'The Beadle of the World' was Douglas Jerrold's description of him, and only those who knew the redoubtable John could understand how admirable a sobriquet it was. Yet a truer friend and a kinder heart it was impossible to conceive. It is clear that Barham disliked if not loathed him. He was 'a low scribbler,' he says, 'without an atom of talent, and totally unused to the society of gentlemen. He narrowly escaped expulsion through publishing an account of a dinner at the Garrick in a newspaper to which he was a reporter. The committee wrote him a letter on the occasion, expressive of their disgust, which would have caused any other man to retire. About a year after he got drunk at the anniversary Club dinner. Tom Duncombe got drunk at the same time, but behaved so differently that Poole observed one was the real gentleman drunk, the other a "spewrious" gentleman drunk. He became subsequently a sort of toady to

Talfourd and Macready, and wrote the theatrical criticisms in the *Examiner*.

Here was Richard Bentley, whose name used to figure in a stately way on his title-pages as 'Publisher in Ordinary to Her Majesty'. He was of the line of Murrays and others, who styled themselves and were styled 'Mr'. There was a strong personal element in his business and this was strongly asserted. It was the same with the old Dickensian house, Chapman and Hall, where each partner was well known and familiar to the community. Richard Bentley succeeded to Colburn of the *New Monthly*, and of Lady Morgan and others. In another fashion the redoubtable John Forster succeeded to Colburn, marrying his widow, the gentle and amiable Mrs Forster, who also brought him many valuable MSS, and literary treasures.

There were three generations of Bentleys, and I knew them all. Richard the first, 'Her Majesty's Publisher in Ordinary,' was a remarkable man in his way, always to be associated, however, with the mistake of having let 'Boz' slip through his fingers. He was acute enough to discover the certain success of the young fellow and had secured him by agreement, but mainly owing to John Forster's diplomacy and pressure, he was induced to let off his victim, as he was considered to be. I must say I think, on the whole, that he behaved well; for he had Dickens bound to him and mortgaged *corps et âme*, but let him go for a consideration. I suppose he saw that, by and by, it would be impossible to have him as a willing worker, and so compounded. I never can forget my own obligation to him and his spirited encouragement – how he read one story of mine and said 'Write me as good a one as that, and I'll give you £150' – and so he did, and many a hundred more. I see him now before me, a little man with a pink face and white prickly hair. I knew also George the son, who was also my friend and supporter; and finally Richard, under whom the business was transferred to other hands.

One of the quaintest and most original of the lively Charles Mathews' jests was his speech at the farewell dinner given to him in 1870, when he himself took the chair! He said, 'I venture to assert, and I think I may do so without vanity, that a fitter man to propose the health of our guest could not be found, for I venture to assert emphatically to affirm, that there is no man so well acquainted with the merits and demerits of that individual as I am. I have been on the most intimate terms with him from my youth. I have watched over and assisted his progress from childhood upwards, have shared in all his joys and griefs, and I assert boldly I am proud to have this opportunity of publicly declaring that there is not a man on earth for whom I entertain so sincere a regard and affection.'

The year is 1884. The father of Beatrix Potter, the children's author–artist, was dining at the Garrick and later recounted a story which found its way into his daughter's secret coded diary: 'Lord Alcester was overheard to remark at the Garrick Club that the French navy is greatly over-rated, he says the service is constantly disorganized though the ships are good. The Italian is much stronger. This same Lord Alcester is a great fop, and is called "The swell of the ocean". He admired a very rich widow, being very poor himself, and, when he got his title, it was supposed she would have him, but did not.'[7]

Malcolm Muggeridge resigned from the Garrick because of a stupid row over a broadcast – an innocuous and rather sensible one – about the monarchy on the Jack Paar show in America. But this was at a time when the Queen was not called 'Brenda' in *Private Eye* and the aura of Queen Mary still hung about the Palace. He used to be a quite frequent Garrick attender. He recalls in his memoirs being asked before the Second World War to undertake a new version of Ian Hay's *The First Hundred Thousand* about the B.E.F. in France.

Thinking about it – the advance proposed was substantial – I could not bring myself to relish the project. It would inevitably mean dishing the war up as some sort of crusade, whereas I saw it as an act of self-destructive desperation on the part of all concerned . . . When, after the war, I was a member of the Garrick Club for some years, I used sometimes to see Ian Hay there; a tall, lantern-jawed, elusive-looking man. I never managed to summon up the courage to tell him that I had been chosen, but declined to pick up in the second world war the torch he had carried in the first. I felt it might upset him.[8]

Satters missed Ian Hay by a few weeks only, but recalls many other notable writers of his time – and theatrical people, of course. He writes:

During the years that I was Secretary of the Garrick Club, ie. from 1st January 1953 to 31st December 1972 (20 years exactly) a great many changes took place and many more have taken place since. All these changes have altered the character of the Club in many ways but not entirely.

Names of those earlier days I remember well are, first those of the theatre: Felix Aylmer, Ivor Brown, George Curzon, Basil Dean, Walter Fitzgerald, Jack Hawkins, Leslie Henson, Alistair Sim, Sir Godfrey Tearle, and those not of the theatre but ardent patrons of it, such as T.S.Eliot, Somerset Maugham, Stephen Potter, Jack Gilroy, Lord Webb-Johnson, Sir Travers Humphreys, Harold Abrahams, 'Plum' Warner and Bernard Darwin.

Twenty years earlier Arthur Pinero, the actor to whom the Garrick owes the most, and whose contribution helped Satters through a worrying financial time, died. The Trustees and one or two others had heard discreetly in 1933 that the Club would benefit by his death, which occurred in November. But this is how members first read of the windfall, though from this they could have no idea of the extent by which the Club would benefit:

SIR ARTHUR PINERO
LEAVES £63,000

£1,000 TO A WOMAN FRIEND:
A SERVANT AS EXECUTRIX

Sir Arthur Pinero, the dramatist, who was 79 when he died last November, left gross estate of £63,310, net personalty £62,898.

Among his bequests was:

'£1,000 to my old friend Laura Taylor, as a mark of gratitude and affection . . .'

For his sisters, Frances Lucy Paine and Mary Ross Pinero, he left an annuity of £400.

He gave his effects not otherwise bequeathed to his step-daughter Myra Hughes, directing her to offer to the National Portrait Gallery the oil painting of himself by Mordecai and to the Garrick Club the marble bust of himself by Emil Fuchs.

He also gave £100 to the Pensions Fund for the servants of the Garrick Club.

The residue of his property he left upon trust for Mrs Hughes for life and on her death £500 to Claude Neville Hughes, and the ultimate residue equally between the Garrick Club, the Royal Literary Fund, and the Middlesex Hospital.

There is a minor thesis to be chosen by some light-hearted post-graduate on unplanned Club members' meetings about the globe, in the most unlikely places. I met Giles Playfair (1933) recently in an airport lounge in Malaysia. We have known one another for years and sat on the general Committee together. But the locale was so remote and unsuited to meeting a familiar face that he did not recognise mine until I was forced to ask him his name. But this is somewhat more dramatic, from Richard Crawshaw:

After my election as a member of the Garrick Club, in 1965, I was given to understand that when my name came up for consideration at the committee meeting and when members of the committee were asked what, if anything, they knew about me The Lord Russell of Killowen's succinct comment was, 'All that I can remember about him is that, on the occasion of the D-Day landing in Normandy, we could not find a slit trench deep enough for him!' He and I were both with the 6th Airborne Division (Air Landing Brigade). We both landed in gliders and both occupied trenches in the same orchard. His comment, of course, was merely to register the fact that he had not forgotten that I am somewhat inordinately tall – 2 metres to be exact. In fact I, myself, was responsible for my own slit trench which, needless to say, was dug deep enough.

Then, in 1945, we both took part in the Airborne landing across the Rhine and, shortly before the end of the war, Lord Russell was wounded at the crossing of the Elbe.

Almost exactly twenty years later they were comparing notes and exchanging drinks; and another twenty years on they are, happily, still doing so.

Satters tells of lunching late at the Club one day with Tony Kimmins and half a dozen others at the small ten-table by the fireplace when another member brought in his guest and pointed proudly to the large pictures on the west wall. 'These are some of the Zoffanys,' he said. The guest, uncertain of his meaning, played it safe, glanced at the table and remarked, 'Well, I guess I mustn't interrupt them at their lunch,' and hurriedly walked out.

That garrulous old gossip, William Stone, had two newspaper stories of around the turn of the century:

A friend of mine among the critics was Joseph Knight of the

Globe and the Athenaeum. He was a well-known member of the Garrick and used to sit there, writing his criticisms, until 3 or 4 a.m., so that the club imposed a fine on anyone staying after 2 a.m. Knight had an old four-wheeler to take him home somewhere in the north of London. He was a very convivial person; you may remember what Max said after spending a long session with him, 'The Knight had a thousand whiskies, I but one.'[9]

We were talking about the *Daily Telegraph*, and I might mention that one day I was in the Garrick Club when Lord Burnham came in. He was driving down to Fleet Street and looked in on the way. One of the members said to him, 'Oh, I suppose a great paper can go on on its own?' 'Not at all,' said Burnham. 'Nothing goes on on its own. I'm going down to give it a push.'[10]

Sir Robert Lusty strikes an unexpected political note in his memoirs, though of the lightest nature. He had met a Russian in New York in connection with his international publishing activities. He met him again in London:

> The Russian Trade Mission staged its mammoth show at Earl's Court. Mezh Kniga's representative in London telephoned me to say that Donev (which was not his name) would be coming. I was mildly surprised, but delighted. We must all meet, I suggested. I asked him to get in touch when a date could be set and I would arrange something with Tom Girtin. 'I do not think there will be time,' he said.
>
> But to our astonishment there proved to be time, for he telephoned a week or so later to say so. An evening was contrived and we collected the two of them from a seedy hotel in the Earl's Court area. First we took them to the Garrick Club for dinner. 'Here,' I explained, 'you can see real communism in action. The members share it all. You have nothing at all like it.' They neither could nor would believe it. It was utterly beyond their comprehension. Old Joan, the greatest character of her day among the waitresses, took them to her capacious heart.

She enchanted them and after dinner they gravely sought her out and thanked her for her care, shaking her warmly by the hand. It was most charmingly done, and a brave gesture in a strange land.[11]

In a land where self-introductions come awkwardly, and in a club where everyone is supposed to know everyone else, there are bound to be occasional curious encounters. Like Duff Cooper's in 1927:

I had a snack at the Garrick on the way to the theatre. During my hasty meal I sat next to a man whom I thought charming. He was humble and shy. We discovered that we had both been in America and discussed the country. Because he was humble I became patronising, and when I left I casually asked the head waiter who the gentleman was I had been sitting next to – 'Mr P. G. Wodehouse'. I wished I had been nicer.[12]

Or the young Bailey-King, Robert. He made polite conversation to his elderly neighbour at dinner, telling him that after five years at Christie's, he found getting back to studying and reading for the bar very confusing. 'I find studying difficult, too,' his neighbour said sympathetically. 'You're reading for the bar, too, are you, sir?' asked Bailey-King, knowing that some retired men do read for the bar for the intellectual stimulation it offered. He was met with a roar of laughter. 'Oh no, dear boy, I'm the Lord Chancellor.' Yes, it was Lord Gardiner, a member since before P. G. Wodehouse's dinner with Duff Cooper.

Chance encounters are one of the special pleasures of club life – 'Well, where on earth have you been since . . .?' Thirty-five years after Brian Aherne had been my every week-end host when I was training for the R.A.F. outside Hollywood, there he suddenly was, as tall and elegant as ever. Back in those days I jitterbugged to the

[115]

music of my swing-god, Benny Goodman, and his gorgeous new young singer Peggy Lee. In walked Benny Goodman one day, looking youthful, as a guest from his New York club; in a trice, Satters introduced him to fellow American Mike Canfield, Alfred Francis and his once-young hero-worshipper. The dry martinis flowed until Benny Goodman remarked, 'Do you *eat* here, too.' And so we did, and a swinging lunch it was.

And these anecdotes can last for as long, but, like the silent wish at some of the Garrick's Shakespeare dinner speeches,

> 'O! that a man might know
> The end of this day's business . . .'
> (Brutus's exhortation)

8

Scandals and Outrages

*'None were right and all were wrong, upon
my life and soul, O demmit!'*

THE BIGGEST SCANDAL in Garrick history stemmed from three
of its writer–members – those 'penny-a-liners', those 'vermin', so
despised by the swells of White's, Boodles, Brooks's and even some
of the Garrick's own hierarchy. They were the utterly disparate
figures of Charles Dickens, William Makepeace Thackeray and
young Edmund Yates. Yates was a Dickens sycophant if ever there
was one, who scribbled for a number of newspapers and periodicals; Thackeray was *not* a Dickens admirer. One of Yates's organs
was the *Illustrated Times* to which he contributed a provocative
column called 'The Lounger at the Clubs', which he used with
embarrassing frequency to sing the praises of Dickens.

In the early summer of 1858 Yates added to his contributions
another column called 'Literary Talk' in the weekly *Town Talk*.
He had published only one column, in which he made slighting
references to Thackeray, when the editor discovered, just before
going to press the following week, that he had miscalculated the
required copy. He summoned Yates to his office urgently and asked
him to extend his column to fill the gap.

What little discretion Yates enjoyed had all been dissipated by
the late hour and, no doubt, by much claret. In a trice he had rattled
off another and this time ferocious attack on Thackeray, a man who
had (he later accepted) always been kind to him and whose only
crime was to be on coolish terms with Yates's beloved Charles
Dickens. Of Thackeray's work Yates wrote that *The Virginians*
was 'unsuccessful', *Esmond* fell 'almost still-born from the press'
and much more of a sharpish nature. As for the poor man's appearance: 'Mr Thackeray's face is bloodless and not particularly
expressive, but notable for the fracture of the bridge of his nose . . .

[117]

His bearing is cold and uninviting; his style of conversation either openly cynical or affectedly good-natured and benevolent; his *bonhomie* is forced; his wit biting . . .' and so on, in the same vein: rich stuff even for that time.

One of Thackeray's friends, Shirley Brooks, suggested that he should, in order to be done with the matter swiftly, write to Yates: 'Dear Yates, Next time you want a guinea write to me and not of me. Yours, etc.' But that was not Thackeray's style at all, unfortunately. Instead he wrote a letter of inordinate length and occupying as much of his time as a ten-guinea article would consume. This is only a bit of it:

> As I understand your phrases, you impute insincerity to me when I speak good-naturedly in private; assign dishonorable motives to me for sentiments wh. I have delivered in public, and charge me with advancing statements wh. I have never delivered at all.
>
> Had your remarks been written by a person unknown to me, I should have noticed them no more than other calumnies: but as we have shaken hands more than once, and met hitherto on friendly terms, (You may write to one of your employers, Mr Carruthers of Edinburgh, & ask whether very lately I did not speak of you in the most friendly manner) I am obliged to take notice of articles wh. I consider to be, not offensive & unfriendly merely, but slanderous and untrue.
>
> We meet at a Club where, before you were born I believe, I & other gentlemen have been in the habit of talking, without any idea that our conversation would supply paragraphs for professional vendors of 'Literary Talk', and I don't remember that out of that Club I ever exchanged 6 words with you. Allow me to inform you that the talk wh. you may have heard there is not intended for newspaper remark; & to beg, as I have a right to do, that you will refrain from printing comments upon my private conversation; that you will forego discussions however blundering, on my private affairs; & that you will henceforth please to consider any question of my personal truth & sincerity as quite out of the province of your criticism.[1]

Other letters flew all over the place. To Charles Kingsley Thackeray pointed out that the Garrick was 'a social institution quite unlike other clubs . . . where men have been in the habit of talking quite freely to one another (in a little room not fifteen feet square★) for this $\frac{1}{4}$ of a century or more. If the penny-a-liner is to come into this sanctum, and publish his comments upon the conversation there held and the people he meets there, it is all over with the comfort and friendliness of our Society . . .'[2]

Yates came back unapologetically on 15 June: 'I cannot characterize your letter in any other terms than those in which you characterize the article which has given you so much offence. If your letter to me were both "slanderous and untrue" I should readily have discussed its subject with you, and avowed my earnest and frank desire to set right anything I may have left wrong, your letter being that it is. I have nothing to add to my present reply.'

In 1858 Thackeray was one of the most revered figures in the Garrick hierarchy, his word was law, and only a handful of members called him 'Thack'. Yates on the other hand had himself (it was widely understood) been elected a member only in memory of his much-loved father, and, strictly speaking, contrary to the Club rules, being under-age. Yates senior – Frederick Henry Yates – had been a founder member, a comic actor who had once played in France to the troops of another fellow founder-member, the Duke of Wellington. Young Yates traded heavily on his father's name and reputation and certainly had a spritely and engaging style about him; but was *not* to be trusted as a journalist-member, as was now being revealed. Nor did he have the good sense and discretion to play the business down, any more than did Thackeray, who now placed the correspondence before the Committee, chaired by Lord Tenterden, with Charles Dickens as one of the members.

Yates was outraged. 'This article may have been in exceedingly bad taste,' he wrote shamelessly, 'but I submit with great deference and subject to the committee's better judgement, that the committee is not a committee of taste'. Nor, it seemed, were 'distortions

★ This was the smoking room in the King Street days.

of the truth' the Committee's business. Lord Tenterden could not agree any more than could Thackeray, or the members of the Committee, except one, Charles Dickens: 'The Committee seems to have gone perfectly mad,' he wrote. 'I really never met with such ridiculous assumption and preposterous imbecility in my life before . . . Upon my soul, when I picture them in that backyard, conceiving that they shake the earth, I fall into fits of laughter.'[3]

But without more ado, the Committee resolved that this sort of thing was 'intolerable in a Society of Gentlemen', and that Yates had better make an ample apology or resign from the Club, 'and if Mr Yates declines to apologise or retire the Committee will consider it their duty to call a general meeting of the Club to consider this subject'.

By this time the momentum was so great that nothing could stop the steamroller of scandal, to the delight of literary and theatre society. There was always a certain amount of malicious satisfaction at the misfortunes of other clubs, and the Athenaeum smoking room especially relished what was going on, agog for the outcome.

Well, of course Yates had no intention of resigning and made this clear enough to bring about a Special General Meeting in King Street at 3pm on 10 July, 1858, which 177 members attended. 'Frightful mess, muddle, complication, and botheration,' Dickens commented, summoning up the image of a witch's broth in full boil.[4]

Feeling against Yates was by no means unanimous. Over the past weeks, Dickens had come to the aid of his admirer and had gained some powerful support from Wilkie Collins, Sir James Fergusson and other influential people. Since the earlier fiery meeting Dickens had attempted to act as a mediator. He trod carefully and gently, but still stood on Thackeray's tender feet, 'and here was the beginning of the estrangement which so unfortunately clouded the latter days of their acquaintance',[5] although there was a reconciliation shortly before Thackeray died.

The first thing all these 177 members heard was a conciliatory letter from Thackeray. 'The debate, as between me and the writer of the newspaper article which has given me offence, is over. I have expressed my opinion of his conduct in terms of at least as "feigned bonhomie". He has replied. The natural consequences have ensued, and our little society has been plunged for five weeks past in a turmoil, in which I regret sincerely I should have had any part.' This was followed by a letter from Yates, which also gave some hope of an agreement. He said he would still not apologise to Thackeray but would 'apologize to you [the Committee] for any unpleasant feeling that I have awakened in the Club . . .'

After this, the Dickens faction moved and seconded a resolution that, in effect, Thackeray having used 'the strongest language' to Yates in protest at the articles, he had thereby waived his right of complaint. To which the Thackeray clique massed together, one imagines, on the side of the room, a veritable ocean of beards and a hive of outraged murmurings, introduced an amendment in six parts, reversing the Dickens resolution, and condemning the prac-tice of 'publishing such articles'. All but one of these resolutions were carried and the meeting broke up with the clear impression that Yates was going to have to resign. It was all over for the young journalist by 20 July when, after Yates's failure to respond to two letters, his name was 'erased' from the list of members. Simultaneously, Dickens wrote to the Committee:

Gentlemen,

As I had the misfortune to differ from you on the whole principle of last Saturday's discussion, and as I cannot take upon myself the very difficult and unsatisfactory functions which you understand to attach to your Body, but which I believe that Body has no right to assume, I beg to resign my seat at your Board.

        I am, Gentlemen,
           with much regret,
           faithfully yours
           (signed) Charles Dickens

Charles Kean was elected to fill the vacancy caused by Dickens's resignation from the Committee. The affair was almost over, but not quite. Dickens tried again to bring about a reconciliation but again failed; the bitterness and hostility were now too deep. Yates threatened to take the Garrick to court, the Garrick (with an abundance of counsels' opinion to call on) was satisfied that there could be no case against it. Then, fearing the worst, the Committee ordered – 'That in the event of Mr Yates attempting to enter the Club, as a member, its officers and servants do treat him in all respects as a Stranger and use all due and proper means to eject him.'

Yates, accompanied by his solicitor, made two attempts to enter the Club. On the second occasion, the Club secretary, Alexander Doland, restrained him with a hand on his shoulder. 'I suppose that is what you want, Mr Yates – will this do?' It did satisfy the solicitor, who left with his client, confident that an offence had been committed because Yates had paid his full subscription for the year and that he was legally the owner of one four hundredth (or so) of the Club. All this got the silly fellow nowhere and nothing, except the warning that his costs if he lost the case would be over £300 – or 72,000 lines at a penny a time. He did not risk it.

The other two 'scribblers' could not resist introducing the chief characters into their next books. Yates's Q.C., Edwin James, whom Dickens had met through Yates, became Mr Tryver in *A Tale of Two Cities* – 'stout, loud, red, bluff, and free from any drawback of delicacy . . .' Thackeray introduced Yates as 'Young Grubstreet' in issue number 9 of *The Virginians* and 'allowed himself a further reference to Bob Bowstreet, Tom Garbage, and the *Kennel Miscellany* in number 11 of *The Virginians* three months later'.[6]

As for Yates himself, he continued to flail about, making disparaging references to Thackeray and to *Punch* which had hotly criticised him. Many other public figures felt his lash until the Earl of Lonsdale got him on libel. He was found guilty and sentenced to four months. It is said he never really recovered from the experience. He was last seen at the Garrick – the theatre – attending a revival of *Money*. Now thin and haggard, he fumbled for his hat as the stalls emptied, stumbled and fell, overcome by a seizure. He died an hour later at the Savoy Hotel. He was a man fated to be on the fringe of things, and fated to be compared unfavourably to his father. All he really left the world – apart from a silly autobiography

– was the pseudonym 'Lewis Carroll', which he suggested to the Rev C.L.Dodgson.

The *cause célèbre* was summed up by Sir Frank Burnand 'that Edmund Yates was wrong to begin with, that Thackeray was wrong to go on with, and that Charles Dickens acted impulsively and rather more hastily than he would otherwise have done, had it been against anyone except Thackeray. To paraphrase Mr Mantalini's summing up, "None were right and all were wrong, upon my life and soul, O demmit!" '[7]

Working chronologically through the records, a reader receives the impression that rudeness and acrimony have diminished over the years, and that the second half of the twentieth century is a millpond of tranquillity and amity by comparison with the mid-nineteenth century at the Garrick. And this is to rely only on *recorded* evidence; heaven knows how many tiffs and snaps and unpaid accounts and flouting of rules took place that have been lost in the cigar clouds of the smoking room. There is no reason to believe that other clubs did not suffer – or in many cases enjoy – this minor internecine warfare. It was mainly a reflection of the social climate and manners when men were commonly more arrogant, outspoken and offered their views on everyone more openly, and had more time on their hands. As for the treatment of the servants, I suspect a member who spoke to a 1985 waiter or waitress in the terms and manner of 1885 would soon be asked to resign. Then what about *borrowing money* from the staff!

On 4 April 1857 Mr Percy Boyd of Ryde, Isle of Wight, received a letter from the secretary rebuking him for not paying his subscription. It was not the first time he had been reminded, and in those days you were 'erased' with less compunction than today. Mr Boyd was 'erased'. Moreover, he was told, the Committee 'regret having to submit some other matters to you which call still more strongly for explanation. It seems that you are in debt to the Steward and two other servants of the Club, a course of conduct which the committee hold to be amongst the most objectionable of which a member can be guilty. Moreover, it is not in your case a casual occurrence . . .' And so on.

Confirmation of guilt is almost always to be found in over-long replies, if the Garrick Committee minutes can be relied upon. Mr Boyd's reply ran for pages; very indignant he was, too, stating that it was common practice among members to use servants as temporary bankers; why, it was done every day. And 'I am anxious for an opportunity for a personal explanation in the presence of whoever has thus misrepresented me.'

That was a very foolish thing to write, for it led to a further enquiry downstairs, which elicited the information, which had been a subject of daily chatter and complaint among the servants, that Mr Boyd had been at it for a long time and more widely than had been discovered earlier. So, in a short, snappy reply the secretary now accused Mr Boyd thus: 'You are at this moment in debt to every single male servant in the Establishment, from the Steward to the Messenger . . .'

Mr Charles Hambro's problem was also a financial one, but with an abject apology he survived erasure, though it was a bad start. He was elected on 19 May 1860, brought in a guest a few days later, dined in the visitors' room and left without paying his bill, his entrance fee or his subscription. This was, in the opinion of the Committee, 'unjustifiable' and 'unprecedented'.

A number of members went bankrupt, which instantly and automatically erased their name from 'the list of members'. This sounds callous but was very necessary as every member had a share in the Club's property and this could have been seized by the court on behalf of his debtors – say, two Zoffanys and a silver goblet or two.

Second to running up debts with the servants, passing dud cheques was also severely frowned upon. There was, for example one John L. Litton, a Dublin barrister and a member also of the Carlton Club when he was elected in January 1868. Not for the first time, he paid for his dinner, plus a sum of cash, with a cheque which bounced. This was on 17 January 1873, in spite of his being warned previously and ordered to pay only in cash. The cheque was returned by Coutts & Co, who added that the account had been closed for some time. On 2 February, Mr Litton received a letter which began ominously, 'Sir, I am directed to inform you that the Committee of this Clubhouse have been made acquainted with the following circumstances . . .' And ending: 'The Committee at a special meeting have unanimously decided that you have placed yourself within the purview of Rule 26 and have accordingly resolved that you have ceased to be a member of this Club . . .'

Then, what about the odd behaviour of Mr Walter Lacy of the Drury Lane Theatre, proposed by no less a figure than 'Papa' Fladgate and supported by a full page of signatures back in the King Street days?

> Garrick Club
> March 6th 1886

Dear Sir,

Complaints have been made to the Committee of your turning down the gas in the Morning Room, and of your covering with paper ventilation there, contrary to the wish of members; I am directed to call your attention to these complaints; the Committee feeling sure that you will not in future act in a manner which interferes with the comfort and convenience of members generally.

> Believe me
> Yours truly
> D. Plunket
> Chairman of Committee

To
Walter Lacy Esq

Mr D. E. Bandman, an actor of Cavendish Square, put up by Tom Taylor, the irascible but waggish dramatist and editor of *Punch*, suffered a heavier burden of trouble than Mr Lacy. 'Mr Bandman is represented to have been summoned for an assault upon a lady which appears in this evening's (20 April 1878) paper,

[125]

and without prejudicing the defence which may be offered I think it right to suggest in case Mr Bandman should be convicted of the offence "that the committee should take the steps incumbent upon them . . .": i.e.: make sure he resigns at once.'

Read letter from Mr Chitty calling attention to the objectionable manner in which Mr Watmore sits over the fire to the exclusion of other members. Committee minutes, 13 December 1897.

The following tiff in 1892, though scarcely on the Dickens-Thackeray-Yates scale, is typical of the crotchiness of members which could break out all too easily. There was a Dr Burney Yeo, who was something big like Consulting Physician at King's College Hospital, author of *Mineral Springs and Climates* (not much in demand at the Garrick), who one evening was sitting quietly and alone in the Visitors' smoking room, when George Tredcroft, who did not know the good doctor, came in and was very rude. Yeo wrote complainingly to the Committee, to whom his letter was read. They in turn wrote to Mr Tredcroft to tell him that they were unanimously of the opinion that an apology was due.

Mr Tredcroft, severely ill from influenza (and presumably in need of a senior physician), wrote contritely from his sickbed:

Dear Sir,
Will you convey to the Committee of the Garrick Club my sincere sorrow that I have in any way annoyed Dr Burney Yeo. What I said to him in the Visitors' Smoking Room was said more in fun than from any disrespect for him. As we did not know each other I could have had no latent motive for discourtesy. We all make mistakes in this world and I am willing to acknowledge that I have made one and therefore apologize to Dr Burney Yeo from my heart . . .
                    I am, dear Sir,
                         Yours faithfully,
                              (signed) George Tredcroft

Half a century later this sort of thing was still going on, but far less frequently than when the Good Queen still reigned – and, incidentally, her nephew, H.S.H. Prince Ernest Leopold Victor Charles Auguste Erich Leiningen was in the chair at the meeting at which Tredcroft's letter was read out. Artists as well as actors and physicians could be the victim of 'unpleasant remarks'. For instance, Robert Lutyens had a particularly nasty evening on 26 February 1948.

I was in the Lounge of the Club, preparatory to dining. Sir Alfred Munnings, amongst others, greeted me in the usual way. I ordered a drink and shortly afterwards went to sit beside him. He had previously been joined by Mr Stanley Morison. They were talking about the Exhibition of Chagall pictures at the Tate Gallery. Sir Alfred was, as might be expected, highly resentful of the prominence given to this painter. I interpolated to the effect that I regarded his work as possessing considerable beauty and exchanged views with Mr Morison who held a contrary opinion, expressing it with studied moderation.

At this stage Sir Alfred allowed himself to indulge in violent abuse of the Curator of the Tate Gallery, Mr John Rothenstein, saying that he was a bloody Jew, which was why he showed the pictures of another one.

Stanley Morison, the distinguished typographer, and Lutyens, protested, leading Munnings to launch a violent and loud attack on Lutyens in particular, claiming that his grandfather had been 'a real painter and a great architect whereas you have built neither cathedrals nor bridges. Why! you are not even an architect.'

Lutyens's letter of complaint resulted in a stern rebuke from the secretary, but, curiously, no demand for an apology. Perhaps they guessed what the answer to that would be, and that the resulting scandal would certainly reach the newspapers: '*Times* man and artist savagely abused by President of Royal Academy . . .'

Today there are so many gossip columnists and so voracious an appetite for trivial scandal that a Munnings affair like that would certainly get out. Thankfully, everybody is so relatively polite and compatible that the penny-a-liners, or five-pounds-a-liners, find little to report except an occasional blackballing, although it has to be said that matter on the notice board and even the general Committee's proceedings sometimes find their way to Fleet Street with amazing speed.

Still, stories can always be fabricated, and from the flimsiest evidence. For instance, Peter Jay recalls a lunch at the Garrick with the incumbent ambassador in Washington, Sir Peter Ramsbottom, just after the announcement that Jay would shortly supersede him. 'The press were at our throats and trying to discover some enmity between us. In fact we were old friends. Sir Peter was smuggled in by a back way by the secretary . . . Afterwards on the steps of the club Sir Peter bent down for a moment to do up his shoelace and was photographed in this posture beside me in what was represented as an attitude of mock obeisance!'

At 35 King Street in the 1830s, in Garrick Street in the 1980s, the curiosity about just what goes on behind the front doors, and who is saying what to whom, never abates. It is flattering to members in a way, but also a damn nuisance! It does, however, give us some small idea of what our Patron has to put up with.

9

Games and Occasions

'*The convivial enjoyment of the evening was upheld with
unabated good humour and pleasantry to the midnight hour.*'
Dinner for the President, 1832

SINCE THE GARRICK Club's primeval days in the 1830s every possible excuse has been seized upon for a celebration, from some sort of anniversary to more regular meetings, like those of The Literary Society, so sharply recounted to Rupert Hart-Davis by George Lyttelton in their published letters from 1955 to 1962:

> The Lit Soc last night produced a fine crowd. The uproar was terrific and prevented my hearing anything my neighbour said to me . . . I sat next to Tommy [Lascelles], and Ivor B[rown] was on my other side. Flash Harry [Sir Malcolm Sargent] was opposite – in cracking form, clearly enjoying himself. Alan Moorehead was very friendly . . .[1]

Today The Naval Historians, including a number of Garrick members, meet annually and others more often. But occasions for Garrick Club members only are more special – like this very early celebration in May 1832:

> On Saturday, a number of members of the Garrick Club gave a farewell dinner to their president, the Earl of Mulgrave, on the eve of his departure for the government of Jamaica. About fifty sat down to dinner; but as this is to be considered rather a private mark of esteem and respect than a public meeting, we forbear going into details. Suffice it to say, that the Earl of Glengall filled the chair, and that the convivial enjoyment of the evening was upheld with unabated good humour and pleasantry to the midnight hour. On his health being drank, Lord Mulgrave addressed the company in an elegant and feeling manner; as did,

at subsequent periods of the entertainment, Lord Glengall, the Marquess of Clanricarde, Mr Frank Mills, Mr Frank Sheridan (who being toasted as the grandson of Richard Brinsley Sheridan, returned thanks in a neat and appropriate speech), Mr Mathews, Mr Sheridan Knowles, and others. The agreeable alternation of song and humorous ballads was happily kept by Duruset, Power, Mathews, and Mathews junior, who chanted one piece as full of pun and point as it could well be stuck. We are inclined to suspect that this smart and amusing composition also owed its authorship to the singer. The party broke up highly delighted with their treat, and only desirous of repeating it on more auspicious occasions than such as the loss of their valued president.[2]

Only a month later there was another dinner, this time to celebrate the retirement from the stage of Charles Young, one of the disciples of the Kemble school of acting:

This most agreeable of clubs gave a dinner on Thursday to Mr Young, on his retirement from the stage. The Marquess of Clanricarde took the chair, and was supported by about sixty members, lovers of the drama, and admirers of their honoured guest. Among the company were Lords Castlereagh, Kinnaird, W. Lennox, Edward Thynne, Henry Fitzroy, and the Hon. Mr Stanley; Messrs Macready, C. Kemble, Farley, Charles Taylor, Sheridan Knowles, Abbott, Harley, Duruset, C. Mathews, &c. &c. Mr Young's health, which was introduced by the noble chairman in an appropriate and pointed speech, was received with enthusiasm; and that distinguished actor returned thanks with feeling and eloquence. The memories of Garrick, of Shakespeare, and of John Philip Kemble, were afterwards given. Charles Taylor sang many humorous songs, and was rewarded with a bumper and three times three. Harley, Duraset, and Charles Mathews, also shewed by their exertions that they were determined not only to enjoy themselves, but also to impart merriment to others. Lord Kinnaird, on the retirement of the Marquess of Clanricarde, took the chair, and the meeting did not separate till a late hour – too late for us to do more than give it this brief notice.[3]

There was another one, for the retirement of Charles Kemble himself from the stage, in January 1837. Not enough room for all who wanted to attend, so off they went to the Albion Hotel, which did well out of the Garrick's big occasions while the Club was still in King Street. 'One hundred sat down under the presidency of Sir Francis Egerton.'

An actor's tour of America or the colonies was sufficient excuse for a party in the mid-19th century, when a sea crossing was quite a business. The 'send-off supper given to J.L.Toole prior to his tour in the Colonies by Ninety Members of the Garrick Club' took place on 18 January 1890 was just one of a number of celebrations of this nature. Irving presided and John Hollingshead, with whom Toole had been associated for a long time at the Gaiety, was among many friends there with whom he had worked.

According to a correspondent in *The Times*:

Toole arrived in a mood of deep depression, which he seemed unable to shake off, even when he rose to return thanks, but then apologetically explained it as due to a dream he had the night before. He had seen himself approaching the gates of Paradise, and, on craving entrance, rebuffed by being told there was 'No admittance for actors'. As he crept away disconsolate, he met Irving making for the same entrance, and warned him to go no farther. Irving thought it well to go on, and, after a word with the keeper of the gate, passed in. That was too much for Toole's sense of impartiality, and he at once retraced his steps and expostulated, only to be met by the gatekeeper's audible whisper, 'That's all right, Irving is no actor'. After that, no doubt good digestion waited on appetite, and the rest of the evening went merrily for the guest of honour and for his hosts.[4]

A life member of the Garrick, Hamish Hamilton, can recall the Pinero dinner of 1928. 'I remember Pinero, much acclaimed, relating that when as a young man he was working as a solicitors' clerk in Lincolns Inn Fields, he would eat his sandwich lunch in the Fields and then make his way to Garrick Street where he would perch on some railings opposite the Club, looking with admiration at Sir John Hare and other stage celebrities, little thinking that many years later [1887] they would propose, second and back him.'

Pinero was by then a Trustee of the Club, with which his whole career as actor and playwright was inextricably entwined. By 1875 Pinero had quit his father's solicitor's office and became an actor in the Edinburgh stock company. Collins was in Liverpool that year attending rehearsals of his play *Miss Gwilt* and searching, as always, for talent for the West End. Impressed by an actor called Pinero, he made enquiries later and was put in touch with his namesake in Edinburgh. As a result, Arthur Wing Pinero came to London and began his association with Irving at the Lyceum.

There is an old chestnut about Irving backstage warning Pinero about some hazardous sharp scenery. 'Careful, or you'll cut yourself.' 'Mr Irving, we are accustomed to having our parts cut in this theatre.'

Then there was the half century celebration of the founding of the Club, the half century celebration of the move to Garrick Street; *and* the 75th, and so on. The centenary dinner on Sunday 22 November 1931 matched up to all these, with the Prince of Wales present as 'an ordinary member'. 'Among those attending,' according to *The Times*, were:

Viscount Burnham, Lord Blanesburgh, Sir Ernest Wild, Sir Max Pemberton, Sir Edwin Lutyens, Sir Arthur Pinero, Sir Milsom Rees, Mr Justice Avory, Mr Cyril Maude, Mr Seymour Hicks, Mr Edmund Gwenn, Mr Henry Ainley, Mr Owen Nares, Mr Lynn Harding, Mr John Drinkwater, Mr A.J. Munnings, RA, Mr Herbert Marshall, Major Ian Hay Beith, Dr Malcolm Sargent.

Guy Boas, in his book *The Garrick Club 1831–1964*, gives a full and moving account of the speech made by Lord Buckmaster on this occasion:

Lord Buckmaster probed the secret of the Club's prosperity.

The intentions of the founders, he stressed, had been loyally adhered to, that Drama remained the central purpose of the Club, and the bringing of its practitioners from suspicious segregation into warm-hearted contact with the outer world. 'But if Drama be regarded as the centre of the Club, yet the physicists tell us that even the most remote atoms of the universe can be resolved into various forms of electrical energy, that the positive element at the centre is called the proton round which the electrons revolve, and so if the Drama be the proton of the Club, there revolve round it with ever varying degrees of velocity and perhaps of importance, the great services of war, commerce, and the law.'

Yet the final factor to which the speaker attributed the Club's success was an element other and larger than Drama, one which delves to the root of happiness in all human intercourse – 'My fellow-members, there is one thing about this Club which we all prize, and it is this, that men here are received at their real value. It makes no difference from where they come, it makes no difference what they do, it does not make much difference, within reasonable limits, what they say; but they must observe a nodding acquaintance with the Rules, which they have never read, and an inflexible fidelity to those other rules which, though never formally enacted, all honourable men think it a shame to violate. It is, therefore, here that old and young, wise and foolish, can all meet together on terms of common equality. Men are measured here on their merits, that are not those of great achievement, nor of glittering success, nor of rank, or wealth, or fame, or power; they are the merits of gaiety and companionship; and upon that platform old and young can alike join hands.'

'I can only trust that when the next century has gone by and our successors meet together to laugh at our old-fashioned follies, our means of transport, our occupations, our amusements, our literature, our art, they will at least remember that we have done our best to cherish and to hand on undimmed that spirit of kindliness and good fellowship which is the life-flame of the Garrick Club.'

More recently we have had the centenary of the first Garrick Street dinner in 1964, special dinners for actors, like Sir John Gielgud's 80th birthday, and even for an actress, Athene Seyler, to show how liberated we are these days. An annual carol service at the Savoy Chapel has been an enormous success, with families pouring back to the Garrick for supper, special provisions and entertainment for the younger children. There has been a soirée or two, to bring back old times, with a small orchestra playing under the stairs, and in 1979 this highly entertaining order of performance:

Sir John Gielgud – Garrick Prologue
Celia Johnson – a piece about David Garrick written by a
                Frenchman
Donald Sinden and Judi Dench – 'Much Ado About Nothing'
Michael Hordern – 'Jumpers'
Maria Aitken – Lady Bessborough's Diary
Polly Hughes – playing the violin
Roland Culver and Nigel Patrick – (the surprise)
Ian Wallace – three songs

In Satters's first year there was a coronation party in the morning room with a very advanced exhibition of technology – screened television. This held everyone so glued that only Satters himself nipped out to watch the real procession pass by in The Strand; and it was a flop for bar proceeds as the only serious drinking was by the aforesaid two wine waiters.

There was another anniversary in 1981 – 150th this time, with Patrick Ide and Sir Edward Pickering working manfully on the preparations for an evening which included a service of thanksgiving and dedication at St Paul's, Covent Garden, a church with which the Garrick has traditionally been closely associated. Two hundred – twice as many as at the first annual celebration in 1832 – turned up, along with the Patron, who replied to William Douglas-Home's toast to the Club.

There were no billiards that night, and, alas, on many ordinary nights either. When Satters was secretary there was billiards (never *snooker*!) every evening, usually starting at about 5 pm and continuing right through until midnight. Stephen Potter was, naturally, as the author of *Gamesmanship*, a powerful participator, and so was Arthur Ransome – 'but you had to be rather careful of him!' one of his contemporaries remarked.

At one time there was a second table upstairs, which was squeezed into an annexe beyond the present billiards room. 'Members are requested to play Pool on the table near the lavatory.' Pool could be played in 1913 for 6d per game for two or three players, *eight* or more, 2s. Billiards was 100-up for 6d. 'Members are requested not to throw the billiard balls on the table.'

The money was put into a conscience box. Recently this was replaced by a coin-in-the-slot light switch, but reasoning that this was yet another disincentive to climbing half way to the stars when the table is so little used anyway, wiser counsels eventually prevailed: so today it is free billiards – or snooker – for the few who can be persuaded to climb and play. The climb *is* an effort, even an impossibility, for older people. In 1961 George Lyttelton, aged 78, searching for a member who had promised to drive him home, was told he was playing billiards. 'I toiled up and found no one. I came down and asked some genial Garrickians in the lounge where the billiard-room was. They told me it was *two* floors up, and added that they never played the game as they couldn't face the ascent. So once again I climbed . . . and not unnaturally found my legs very achey and twitchy in bed that night . . .'[5]

There is no doubt that the Garrick is not as sporty as it was, by a very wide margin. In the 1940s the present bar and the present reading room next door – the site of the first bar – were occupied by bridge (earlier whist) players, fifteen or even twenty tables sometimes. As bridge declined, in spite of the efforts of the much-loved Frankie Ratto, drink arose in ascendancy and consumption, first driving the diminished number of players out of the smaller room, and finally out altogether. For the past fifteen years, card players have been displaced persons in an increasingly non-sporting club, finally finding refuge in a sort of mis-shapen attic in which have been squeezed two tables, both rarely occupied.

Garrick members are now not even very strong on *spectator* sport. Twenty years ago there would be nudging, squeezing competition to get a chair with a view of the television set showing the second day of the final test against Australia. In 1985 during the final of the televised Benson and Hedges at Lords, there will be two members in front of the 3.45 at Kempton Park. Both will be asleep after a heavy and largely liquid lunch. No wonder the Club's finances, if not members' livers, are in such fine shape.

Satters, like every good retired naval officer and himself a great sportsman, arrived for the first time in the secretary's office on a Monday in January 1953. The next day, the chairman of the house committee, Sir Neville Pearson, said, 'Commander, you had better come to the meeting on Thursday and act as secretary.' He did so. The agenda was promptly dealt with. 'Any other business?' asked the chairman.

'I've got an idea, sir,' said Satters. 'Has the club ever thought of running a trip to the Derby?'

'Yes, we did once, and it was a complete failure.'

Satters pressed the point, mentioning that he had done it several times in the navy and always found it was a success.

The committee remained doubtful, and someone said, 'You won't get a bus now – too late – they'll all be booked.'

'I've already reserved one,' announced the Commander.

That was 1953, and the outing *was* a success, confirmed by Lord Webb-Johnson, one of the Trustees who came along. The numbers increased fast after that, and all through the '50s and '60s it was for many the high point of the Garrick year. Three open-top buses pulled up outside the club-house after members, wives and sometimes older children had eaten breakfast in the coffee room, and off the party went, along with Coleman, two bartenders, a very great deal of champagne and a cold table which showed even Coleman at his best. The buses were high on Epsom Downs by 11 o'clock, and the party continued until about 5.30 pm, intermittently and not seriously interrupted by the racing.

The first time I went, there was a post-luncheon raid on the bar by members of a pub-club from Southend, who made off with bottles of gin and whisky, threading their way through the crowd. They were pursued by elderly, near-toothless 'Nobby' Clark and the gigantic figure of Sebastian Earl, who beat the robbers over the head with champagne bottles, forcing them to yield up their loot, without too much damage to themselves, although 'Nobby' was not behind the bar at the Garrick for a few days after that.

Today the lustre has dimmed with the loss of numbers, and it is all that the secretary can do to fill a single bus, mainly with business-men and their guests. Perhaps it will stage a revival,* like a good vintage play, and we shall witness again scenes like the one so joy-fully depicted by Jack Gilroy in his painting, with Barker dancing a *pas-de-deux* with a member's wife; and Clapham Common at 6 pm and Trafalgar Square at 6.30 pm will echo to the sound of lusty song from the open decks of three buses, streaming scarves and favours of pink and green.

* There are favourable signs in 1985 that it will.

10

Curtain Call

IN 1985 THE GARRICK is at full stretch. There are 940 full members, 176 supernumery members and 22 life members. There are so many people in the candidates' books that severe restrictions have had to be applied to the proposing of new names. There are something like 800 functions at the Club every year, varying from small dinners in the private rooms to cocktail parties and receptions for a hundred guests or more. Every week-day the bar is packed before lunch, to the extent that the hard-of-hearing have to retire in order to carry on a coherent conversation.

The staff, as we have seen, are in fine fettle. The Garrick, in short, is still (as a member noted in 1868) 'a very jolly place to be in'. All the same, it is a very different Club from twenty-five years ago, and scarcely recognisable from the Garrick of 1935. The expansion and the thriving finances have been achieved at a price. The membership has increased so swiftly that old members do not recognise a number of the faces about them: even Tony behind the bar is occasionally baffled.

There are too many businessmen guests and others about the place, especially at lunchtime, brought here for non-social reasons. And some of them are reluctant to be parted from their business cases. Why, one wonders? There is too much political, publishing and media in-chat from which other members are pointedly excluded. Ever since 1832 there have been leaks and indiscretions; all the same, today confidentiality seems almost an old-fashioned anachronism, and you certainly find yourself saying, 'Between you and me . . .' or some such.

It should not be like that. It should not be that a major indiscretion – as happened recently – should be treated as lightly as it was by the Committee because there were so many fellow journalists sitting on it. A request to resign might be a sharp example, and lead to an end to Garrick tittle-tattle appearing all over the place.

And the future? There have been grey periods when the place got pompously above itself and platitude was more in evidence than noisy controversy, and, like the Vicar of Wakefield, the Club was unable to furnish members with argument and intellect, too.★

Too much adulation promotes the multiplication of little gnawing beasts that weaken any works or form of man, from famous judges and actors (same thing?) to a self-satisfied, too easily successful, political party. I suspect the Garrick was over pleased with itself at about the same time that the Victorian navy was being rumbled by that fiery admiral, 'Jackie' Fisher – and wouldn't he have made a great member!

The body corporate of the Garrick is in fine shape just now, in the mid 1980s, and there can be little doubt that the Garrick will remain a pleasant and sought-after Club. But like any organism or organization, there will be changes. To ensure that the changes are for the better and not for the worse, there will still have to be 'very vigilant care for it is clear that it would be better that ten unobjectionable men should be excluded than that one terrible bore should be admitted'; just as there was in 1872.

The quality of life in the Garrick ten years hence, as always, must depend very much on the elected officers and the Trustees – God bless 'em. Old members will testify that it is always surprising how swiftly the tone and special quality – to say nothing of the food – of the Garrick can change.

After reading in the minutes, and more graphically in volumes of letters, diaries and memoirs, of members' formal and informal functions back in the King Street days – of musical evenings, sketches, songs and general community jollification – it would be pleasant to enjoy a return to more of the same thing, and to hear more often the click of ivory balls up in the billiards room and the murmur of 'three no trumps' from the card room.

★ 'I find you want me to furnish you with argument and intellect too. No Sir, there I protest you are too hard for me.'

Inevitably, the question of full membership for women will come up. There seems, for better or worse, little chance of a vote in favour at present. But as night follows day, even in Garrick Street, the subject will be aired from time to time in the future. Or perhaps, if offered full and equal membership, women will not want it.

Meanwhile, to hark back to 15 February 1832: and at about a quarter to nine in the evening, with one hundred and ten founder members of the Garrick dining together for the first time, Barham raises his glass of excellent pre-Waterloo port, gives a toast, and breaks into song, concluding:

> ... Alack! my timid muse would quail
> Before such thievish cubs
> But plumes a joyous wing to hail
> Thy birth, fair QUEEN (or ACE) of CLUBS

Works of Art

THE GARRICK CLUB has a large collection of works of art. There are a number of masterpieces but the collection is remarkable, not so much for the quality of its portraits, as for its comprehensive coverage of the stage and performances, particularly between the mid eighteenth and the end of the nineteenth century. A certain number of portraits of other distinguished members have been added over the years. We are indebted to Guy Boas, the Honorary Librarian of the Club 1952–60, for his recording of the origins of the collection in his book on the Club first published in 1948.

During the second half of the eighteenth century, Thomas Harris, who had been manager of the Covent Garden Theatre, collected theatrical pictures including works by Zoffany, Hayman and Dupont. A large part of his collection was dispersed in 1819 and a number of pictures were bought by the actor, Charles Mathews (1776–1835) who was already an active collector of theatrical pictures. He and his actor son, Charles James Mathews (1803–1878) were among the original members of the Club.

Mathews senior housed his collection at his home, Ivy Cottage, Highgate, and when more space was needed, he employed his son, a pupil of Pugin, to design a gallery in which the collection could be displayed. He had considerable success in the profession but throughout his life he had a series of misfortunes and in 1833 he was forced by financial difficulties to sell his home and the collection. In connection with the sale, it was shown to the public in the Queen's Bazaar in Oxford Street.

Mathews had hoped that the Club would buy the collection but the Club was not able to offer a reasonable price, nor was it sold at the exhibition which ended with a loss of £150. His son had put together a catalogue and, in 1835, Robert Durrant, whose generous attitude towards the Club is mentioned on page 17, described by Guy Boas as 'a self-made stockbroker, a devotee of the theatre and a man of generous idealism' bought all the pictures for £1,000 and lent them to the Club, who still could not afford to buy them. Durrant then gave them to the Club.

Charles James Mathews was an actor of vitality with ability to represent a wide variety of characters. In 1879, the year after his death, 116 water colours of him in numerous roles by James Warren Childs were presented to the Club by Robert Walters, who was the compiler of the first catalogue of the Club's pictures. These water colours hang in the billiard room together with a fascinating oil of 43 identified members in the billiard room, painted in 1869 by Henry Nelson O'Neil, ARA.

No other collections have been acquired by the Club but there is and has always been much affection for the Club and many works have been given by Members, some of whom have been the artists themselves. A recent example is John Gilroy, RA, a member for thirty years prior to his death in 1985, who painted a number of members including a cartoon of the outing to the Derby in 1967. Gilroy was Chairman of the Works of Art Sub-Committee from February 1970 to February 1975.

A full catalogue of the collection is in the course of preparation by Dr Geoffrey Ashton, Honorary Librarian of the Club, and this promises to be of great interest and value. It is impossible to give an exhaustive and full description of the collection. It seems best to limit this appendix to certain artists, categories of work and characters portrayed. Inevitably this is affected by the personal reactions of the writer. Members and visitors will find other works which particularly appeal to them.

One must start with the pictures by John Zoffany (1725–1810) who was born in Germany and, after studying in Rome, came to England at the age of 25. After working for a clockmaker decorating clock faces, he became an assistant to Benjamin Wilson. Garrick, when being painted by Wilson, realised that a talented assistant had painted some of the picture and having made contact with Zoffany, he helped him towards recognition. Zoffany in due course became a Royal Academician and had much success. He spent some time in London. There is a large picture by him in the Victoria Memorial, Calcutta, showing himself at a canvas with a number of prosperous British residents. The Club has ten of his pictures (of which 'The Clandestine Marriage' in the Coffee Room is the grandest) all being theatrical scenes or personalities, including an enchanting sketch of Garrick's head against an unfinished background; the lively vitality is remarkable.

Excellent examples of the work of other artists of this period are in the collection. There are fourteen pictures by George Clint, ARA (1770–1854), twelve by George Henry Harlow (1787–1819), twenty by Gainsborough Dupont (1754–1797). The artist represented by the greatest number of works is Samuel de Wilde (1748–1832) who was of Dutch origin. There are many fair sized canvases and something approaching one hundred and fifty small portraits, many of which hang on the back staircase and, since an anonymous member had them all cleaned, look excellent. In fact, the pictures by this artist in the Club establish his reputation as a splendid painter, his theatrical scenes falling only slightly short of those by Zoffany.

At this point, the writer suddenly realises with embarrassment that he has launched into recording the artists represented in the collection whereas the purpose of the collection is to represent plays and actors. It is perhaps to be expected that Shakespeare's plays should be the most frequent subjects. Two of Coriolanus, eleven of Hamlet, two of Julius Caesar, ten of the various King Henrys, three of King John, one of King Lear, ten of Richard III, nine of Macbeth, four of the Merchant of Venice, nine of The Merry Wives of Windsor, two of Othello, five of Romeo & Juliet, one of the Tempest and three of Twelfth Night. There are also scenes or characters from plays by Ben Jonson, Dryden, Gray, Garrick himself, Vanburgh, Otway, Sheridan, Pinero, Congreve and many others.

Actors, actresses and authors are represented in large numbers and it is only possible to allude to a comparatively few. There are not only enormous oil paintings such as the vast canvas by Mather Brown of 'The Gamester', a tragedy by Edward Moore written in 1753, but also a myriad of small works, for instance the endearing little drawing by Sir Thomas Lawrence, PRA, of Mrs Siddons *en profil* in a bonnet with one ravishing dark eye. There is a gigantic landscape of Baalbec given by the artist, David Roberts, RA, to the Club in 1847 and a lively marine painting presented to the Club ten years later by Clarkson Stanfield, RA. The Club also owns a small portrait by Sir John Gilbert, RA, of Thackeray sitting in the Club with the Stanfield picture in the background. There are numerous pictures of Garrick by Zoffany, Worlidge, de Louther-bourg, de Wilde and others and one of the celebrated sculptor Roubiliac working on a bust of Garrick.

It is hard to think of any celebrated actor or actress who is not represented. The galaxy includes John Philip Kemble, Charles Kemble, Charles Mathews and his son, Charles James Mathews, Grimaldi, Sir Henry Irving (a noble portrait by Millais and a wicked caricature by Max Beerbohm), Sir Squire Bancroft, J.L. Toole, Sir Charles Wyndham, Sir John Hare, W.H.Kendal, Allan Aynesworth, Sir Herbert Beerbohm Tree, Sir George Alexander, Sir Gerald du Maurier, Granville Barker, Arthur Bourchier, Sir John Martin-Harvey, Sir Johnston Forbes-Robertson, Sir Arthur Pinero, Anthony Hope, Sir James Barrie, Owen Nares, W. Somerset Maugham, Sir Seymour Hicks, Leslie Howard, Alistair Sim, Sir Donald Wolfit, Lord Olivier, Ben Travers, Sir Noel Coward, Sir John Gielgud and Sir Lewis Casson.

Among the ladies, Nell Gwyn, Peg Woffington, Mrs Siddons, Dame Ellen Terry, Mrs Patrick Campbell, Dame Marie Tempest (a charming portrait by Jacques Emile Blanche), Lilian Braithwaite, Dame Gladys Cooper, Dame Edith Evans, Constance Cummings and Isabel Jeans, not to mention an actress with the fascinating name of Mrs Bracegirdle.

Not only does the Club own this large collection of pictures but also much sculpture. On the first floor landing there is an imposing bronze of Irving by Courtney Pollock, RBA, two busts by Epstein of Franklin Dyall and Dame Sybil Thorndike and a marble head of Sir Arthur Pinero, behind which hangs an impish caricature of him by Sir Max Beerbohm. In the Milne Room there is an endearing bust of Ellaline Terriss in white marble but with a silver collar, by Albert Toft.

There are numerous miniatures and Victorian tinsel pictures. The recital (by no means all embracing) of this panorama of theatrical personalities will remind some members of the safety curtain which used to grace the London Coliseum in which a whole crowd of characters were shown, ranging from Shakespeare to Nijinsky and Grock. This was a source of fascination and pleasure to many, as indeed is the Club's collection.

The Club is a treasure-house in which there are some surprises. When some years ago a lot of re-hanging was being carried out, a large brown paper parcel under the billiard table was found to contain a complete set of Hogarth's engravings with only one missing. During the re-hanging a large and important portrait of Garrick was found very dirty and almost invisible over the telephone box and has been hung in the Bar. A large cupboard of prints and drawings was opened up in the basement. Some of these are now hanging, the rest being kept in Solanders.

The Club is proud of this large collection and over recent years has allocated an annual allowance for their care. Gradually all the pictures and their frames are being cleaned and restored but with so many it is a never ending task similar to painting the Forth Bridge. The lighting has been considerably improved. The Club is constantly asked to lend pictures to exhibitions or to make them available for study.

A major problem is the addition of new works which are so often generously offered. Should the Club always welcome additions so that to some extent this pageant of the theatre should be kept up to date?

A factor which cannot be ignored is that of space. Every room, every wall and every staircase, lavatory and corridor is playing to capacity. With great effort, everything has been hung somewhere. It has now been decided that the Club will accept with pleasure gifts of portraits of actors and actresses but with the limitation that they must be of pre-eminent players and be works of a quality to merit inclusion in the collection. Indeed, it is possible that the Club may, from time to time, when funds permit, commission portraits of the really outstanding players of the day.

There is also a considerable collection of memorabilia, mostly shown in cabinets. These have a nostalgic charm of their own having been worn or used by legendary theatrical figures. Garrick's fishing rod may well be that appearing in the Zoffany picture of him fishing in the Thames-side garden of his grand villa at Hampton. The villa and garden are still there but, alas, now bisected by a busy road. Also his powder puff (not swansdown but an actual puffer), his Mess sword and some of his table silver. To his Viennese dancer, Mrs Garrick, belonged the ivory disc, permitting her coach to enter Park Gates.

Again imagine the ravishing Sarah Siddons wearing the pretty coral filet or the authority with which Sir Henry Irving blew his dog whistle. You can envisage Charles Kean fastening the enormous dog collar round his patient St Bernard's neck, or speculate on the circumstances surrounding the gift of an elegant dog collar by Edward VII to the glamorous Gertie Millar.

From more recent times, there are Noel Coward's scent spray and cigarette boxes belonging to Alistair Sim and Kenneth More. A number of walking sticks on which the great leaned, and many pretty miniatures.

Among the Club's own possessions an 1880* menu to wonder at: Oysters; Turtle Soup; Sole; Haggis; Cassoulette de Foie Gras; Saddle of Mutton; Bécasse; Pudding; Caviare. Our predecessors of 100 years ago deserve our respect as well as our envy.

ANTHONY LOUSADA

* Club Dinner.

APPENDIX B

The Library

THE GARRICK CLUB LIBRARY is small but its seven and a half thousand volumes constitute one of the major sources for the study of British theatre history. It has a mass of manuscript material, one of the largest collections of playbills in the world, a number of unique titles and one of the best collections of eighteenth and nineteenth century play texts. There is a large collection of iconographic material to complement the Club's great collection of pictures and the group of old theatrical periodicals is extremely valuable.

The importance of the Library belies the fact that its creation has been haphazard and its survival, at times, precarious. The afterthought added to the original aims of the Club, '. . . and for the formation of a Theatrical Library,' often causes members a moment of bemused confusion and the original members were evidently at a loss when the time came to do something about their aim. The first gesture was made by John Adolphus at the General Meeting on 15 October 1831 when he suggested, 'That the members present their duplicate Dramatic Works to the Club towards forming a library.' The gifts trickled rather than poured in and from 1835 to 1845, *pour encourager les autres*, the more imposing and expensive presentations were published in the lists of members.

James Winston, the first secretary of the Club, was one of the principal early benefactors and his gifts included his own *Theatric Tourist* and the early nineteenth century minutes of the Theatre Royal, Drury Lane. In 1835 he instituted a custom still practised when, in *Rules and List of Members*, he suggested that, 'In order to promote the formation of the Library referred to in the Rule No. 1, all Members are invited to present any works published by themselves or others, suited to the purpose, which the Club will thankfully acknowledge.' Unfortunately, the early correspondence of the Club does not survive but there is a manuscript list of the presentations from 1832 to 1843.

The same manuscript includes a list of library purchases from 1832 to 1836, the first for 10/6 on 19 November 1832 from Thomas Wilson of St Paul's Churchyard was, 'Walker's *Pron. Dict*^{y}. & *Key*,' a book evidently purchased for the benefit of those actor members anxious to acquire the literate gloss so necessary in the company of gentlemen. The early purchases were mostly works of reference but there was also a deliberate policy of building up the collection of plays; it was left to theatrical members, Charles Kemble and Charles Mathews among them, to provide more exciting material such as playbills and manuscripts.

By 1861, when the first manuscript catalogue of the Library was made, the Garrick Club already had an extensive collection of theatrical literature. However, it was basically a very good Library of play texts, including large groups of French and German plays. Library purchases in the mid-nineteenth century are rather a mystery but accounts start again in 1887 and, in part, continue up to 1917. The one guinea Library Fee charged new members from 1864 brought the Library a modest regular income and some of the greatest treasures were bought in the late 1880s and 1890s for derisory sums. For instance, John Rich's account book for Lincoln's Inn Fields and Covent Garden theatres was bought from Maggs in 1888 for three guineas. At the same time the Library built up its collection of important early theatrical periodicals, the seventeen volumes of *The Theatrical Inquisitor* with its charming plates by Samuel De Wilde and others were bought in 1888 for £9.5.0. There was something of a falling off at the turn of the century although missed opportunities were made up in 1912 when amongst a group of play texts, five plays by Oscar Wilde were bought for 25/-.

The Library Fee became worth progressively less and less until in 1982, when it was dropped altogether, the sum raised was barely enough to buy a single book. Today, the Library is financed directly from the Club general account and a modest sum is devoted to filling gaps in the collection and purchasing theatrical reference books.

However, although the Library must attempt to keep up to date to be of any use as a source of reference its main importance lies in its historical collections. The condition of most of the books in the Library was so bad by the early 1960s that they were largely unusable; a couple of pages turned produced instant disintegration. The dispersal of the entire Library was considered and a detailed valuation was made. Fortunately, largely through the efforts of Sir Julian Hall, the Chairman of the Library Committee, only a part of the Library was sold and the remainder was subjected to a strenuous reorganization. Dorothy Anderson was appointed librarian and she applied the standards of the British Museum to the cosy confusion of the Garrick Library. She divided the books into clearly definable sections, replaced the manuscript catalogue with a series of card indexes and generally produced order out of chaos. The condition of many of the books was still a major problem but Sir Julian's last act of generosity to the Library, a legacy of £6,000, meant that several hundred volumes of plays and periodicals could be rebound. In recent years the policy of rebinding has continued and a brighter economic situation has meant that fine half-leather bindings have been commissioned rather than the prosaic buckram of former years. The most important rebinding project, over one hundred folio and elephant folio volumes of Covent Garden and Drury Lane playbills, was completed by the end of 1985. The play-bills have been bound in half-morocco and mounted on acid free paper with water soluble paste. Thus the condition of an extremely important collection has been stabilized while the appearance of the Library has been considerably improved.

Collections such as the rebound playbills make the Garrick Library the very special place that it is and a quick mention of a few of its treasures will serve to emphasize its importance. The earliest manuscripts, dating from the late seventeenth century, relate to the actors and actresses of the Theatre Royal, Drury Lane, whereas the major eighteenth century manuscripts are the Lincoln's Inn Fields account book already mentioned and account books for Covent Garden from the 1750s. The good collection of original David Garrick material includes letters, deeds and contracts as well as the two time books which give, to the minute, the duration of each act of each play in which Garrick performed. C. B. Smith's ten volume compendium of autograph letters includes items to and from all the major figures of the British theatre in the late eighteenth and early nineteenth centuries and there are no fewer than five volumes of material devoted to Drinkwater Meadows, the most prolific theatrical letter writer of the nineteenth century. Other manuscript materials includes the minutes of the Theatre Royal, Drury Lane for almost the whole of the nineteenth century and a unique series of theatrical costume accounts in which costumes for such figures as Macready and Phelps are itemised and costed, button by bow.

The Library contains a number of important collections devoted to single actors, the most significant being Sir Henry Irving's four volume Garrick collection and the twenty-two volumes devoted to Irving himself and collected by his biographer, Percy Fitzgerald. However, there are also a number of extra-illustrated biographies of actors and actresses as well as a four volume Macready collection and an elephant folio devoted to the one-man shows of Charles Mathews, the founder of the Garrick collection of pictures.

The most important iconographic collection is Charles Mathews's own collection of theatrical mezzotints, bound in five volumes and kept in their own case. However, the various collections in the Library include several thousand theatrical engravings. For instance, John Nixon's fascinating two volume collection on the London theatre contains a large number of rare prints as well as original drawings and early theatrical ephemera such as benefit tickets and playbills. Of course, the Covent Garden and Drury Lane playbills, practically complete from 1798 to 1840, are by far the most important group in the Garrick Library but there is also a complete run of Haymarket playbills from 1795 to 1813 as well as series from some of London's minor theatres. The collection of programmes has been rehoused recently in acid-free boxes and is particularly strong in pre-1914 examples.

The vast quantity of material devoted to performance history is backed up by the collection of play-texts, always a major feature of the Garrick Library. The 5,000 titles include a respectable number of seventeenth century editions as well as perhaps the finest collection in existence of early nineteenth century titles. The most important single collection of plays is undoubtedly the series of prompt copies prepared for Covent Garden by John Philip Kemble and presented to the Garrick by his brother Charles. However, the Library also houses a number of eighteenth and nineteenth century dramatic manuscripts, the manuscript of James Barrie's *The Will*, the typescript of Harley Granville Barker's *The Voysey Inheritance* and a vast collection of play scripts and other material presented to the Garrick by Arthur Pinero.

Other areas well covered by the Garrick Library include theatre architecture and the theatrical periodicals already mentioned; the Garrick's copy of *The Era* is complete from 1858 to 1939 and in itself makes the Garrick Library an important centre for theatre research.

GEOFFREY ASHTON

Source References

Chapter 1   *Bricks and Mortar* (p. 13 to p. 31)

1   T. Girtin, *The Abominable Clubman* (1964) p. 19
2   *News and Sunday Herald*. Quoted Girtin p. 33
3   T. H. S. Escott, *Club Makers and Club Members* (1914) p. 48
4   Unidentified newspaper article, October 1831
5   ditto
6   *Oxford Companion to the Theatre*
7   Unidentified press cutting c. 1864 recalling the old premises at the time of the opening of the new club house.
8   Minutes 22 March 1845
9   Minutes 10 March 1848
10 Sean O'Casey, *Rose and Crown* (1952) p. 19

Chapter 2   *Committees* (p. 32 to p54.)

1   J. Timbs, *Clubs and Club Life of London* (1872) p. 49
2   Minutes 25 January 1917
3   ,,   22 June 1916
4   ,,   22 November 1917
5   ,,   11 July 1918
6   ,,   30 January 1919
7   *ibid*
8   Minutes 25 April 1915
9   ,,   18 March 1915
10   ,,   16 March 1916
11   ,,   22 November 1917
12 A. Cooper (ed.), *A Durable Fire: the letters of Duff and Diana Cooper 1913–1950* (1983) p. 49
13 Minutes 21 February 1918
14   ,,   2 May 1918
15   ,,   22 November 1961

Chapter 3   *Members* (p. 55 to p. 68)

1   O'Casey pp. 24–5
2   *Oxford Companion to the Theatre*
3   G.P.Bancroft, *Stage and Bar* (1939) pp. 28–9
4   O'Casey p. 22
5   *ibid* p. 25
6   Percy Fitzgerald, *The Garrick Club* (1904) p. 43
7   *Oxford Companion to the Theatre*
8   Fitzgerald p. 43
9   G.R.Ray, *Thackeray: the Age of Wisdom 1847–1863* (1958) p. 167
10   Fitzgerald p. 59
11   *Irish Times* 20 July 1911
12   Fitzgerald p. 40
13   *ibid*
14   R.Barham, *The Garrick Club* (1896) p. 30
15   *Oxford Companion to the Theatre*
16   *ibid*
17   *ibid*
18   Fitzgerald p. 200
19   F.Burnand, *Records and Reminiscences* (1904) ii pp. 18–9
20   G.Boas, *The Garrick Club 1831–1964* (1964) p. 66
21   Letter to the author, 15 April 1985
22   Burnand p. 313
23   Fitzgerald p. x

Chapter 4   *Encore* (p. 69 to p. 82)

1   W.L.Courtney, *The Passing Hour* (n.d.) p. 190 *et seq*
2   J.Gielgud, *An Actor in his Time* (1979) p. 00
3   C.Chaplin, *My Autobiography* (1964) p. 292

Chapter 5   *Staff* (p. 83 to p. 94)

1   Minutes 4 December 1930
2   ,,   2 May 1940
3   ,,   2 October 1940
4   Garrick Library Scrapbook
5   R.Lusty, *Bound to be Read* (1975) pp. 135–6, p. 287

Chapter 6   Food and Drink (p. 95 to p. 103)

1   Escott p. 255
2   Minutes 21 July 1860
3   ,,   7 January 1865
4   *Evening News* 24 January 1918
5   J. Timbs, *Curiosities of London* p. 107

Chapter 7   Skits and Sketches (p. 104 to p. 116)

1   Sir Squire and Lady Bancroft, *The Bancrofts: Recollections of 60 Years* (1909) p. 372
2   W. Stone, *The Squire of Piccadilly* (1951) p. 76
3   *ibid*
4   *Cooper Letters* p. 132
5   *ibid* p. 154
6   Stone p. 11
7   E. Linder (ed.), *The Journals of Beatrix Potter* (1966) p. 118
8   M. Muggeridge, *The Infernal Grove* (1973) pp. 10–11
9   Stone p. 28
10 *ibid* p. 54
11 Lusty p. 241
12 *Cooper Letters* p. 246

Chapter 8   Scandals and Outrages (p. 117 to p. 128)

1   Ray p. 280
2   *ibid*
3   *ibid* p. 283
4   *ibid*
5   Fitzgerald pp. 67–68
6   Ray p. 284
7   E. Yates, *Records and Reminiscences* (1904) ii p. 13

Chapter 9   Games and Occasions (p. 129 to p. 137)

1   R. Hart-Davis (ed.), *The Lyttelton-Hart-Davis Letters* vi (1984) p. 31
2   Unidentified newspaper May 1832
3   ,,   ,,   2 June 1832
4   *The Times* 13 March 1932
5   Lyttelton-Hart-Davis vi pp. 81–2

Index